Color-Coded Guitar Fretboard Mnemonics

Paul Masterdon

Copyright © 2025 Paul Masterdon
All rights reserved.

No part of this publication may be reproduced, stored in a retrieval system,
stored in a database and / or published in any form or by any means,
electronic, mechanical, photocopying, recording or otherwise,
without the prior written permission of the publisher.
This system is copyright protected.

First published 2025 by Cosmic Jive Publishing

www.cosmicjivepublishing.com
info@cosmicjivepublishing.com

ISBN 978-1-918219-21-0

Also by Paul Masterdon:

Every Good Boy Plays Guitar Fast - for Sight-reading
(Hacks to read music fast, including those pesky ledger line notes)
ISBN 978-1-918219-18-0

Every Good Boy Deserves Fretboard Mastery
(For ultimate Fretboard mapping using color *and* mnemonics)
ISBN 978-1-918219-17-3

All Cows Eat Great Mnemonics (The Scientific Notes)
ISBN 978-1-918219-16-6

Ear Training for Guitarists - coming 2026!

About the Author

The author is a UK-based music educator with a passion for making learning fun and accessible. With years of experience teaching students of all ages, they've discovered that the best way to master music is by engaging the imagination—because when learning feels like play, the notes just stick.

When not crafting quirky mnemonics or demystifying sheet music, they can usually be found tinkering with half a dozen instruments, drinking far too much tea, and insisting that yes, even you can know your way around the fretboard.

This book is their way of sharing the shortcuts, tricks, and "aha!" moments that turn frustration into fluency—one silly mental image at a time.

Colour Code

Amber for A

Blue for B

Crimson for C

Damson for D

Emerald for E

Fawn for F

Gold for G

🎨 Welcome to The Color Guitar Fretboard

The Visual Reference Based on Pure, Logical Color Mnemonics

Thank you for choosing this book. The **Color Edition** transforms the guitar neck into a **clear, logic-based visual map** designed for pattern recognition and quick, uninterrupted reference.

The key to its power is the **Color-Mnemonic System**:

- Blue for B, Crimson for C, and so on.
- This simple but powerful association creates a **direct memory hook**, bypassing the need for complex stories or rote memorization.

This edition is a streamlined, visual-first tool for students who prefer to see musical structure immediately. By focusing purely on this consistent, logical color system, it delivers an uncluttered view of all notes (0–12 frets) that is ideal for advanced theory work and rapid visual analysis.

How This Book Connects to the Complete Guitar Mnemonics System

This book is part of the broader *Guitar Mnemonics System*—a structured approach to mastering musicianship through memory and connection.

- **Focus of this book (The Color Edition): Pure Color Logic.** This edition with the powerful, built-in memory cues of the Color-Mnemonic system.
- **The Full Mnemonics Edition:** This companion book offers another powerful learning path, specializing in the fastest recall by integrating color, characters and storytelling for each fretboard note, including sequence mnemonics for remembering up and down each string and fret.
- **The Larger System:** The complete system also includes titles covering Sight-Reading, Ear Training, and Chord Mnemonics, each reinforcing a unique part of your musical brain (Visual, Spatial, Aural, Conceptual).

Choose the book that fits your learning style. This streamlined visual reference stands confidently on its own, providing you with lasting fretboard fluency in a format that is less expensive than many posters and bigger than any app.

Now, Let's Step Into the Color and Start Exploring. 🎸

the fretboard chart

The notes on the fretboard repeat in the exact same sequence after fret 12 - just one octave higher.

You could kind of consider your axe being 'cut' in half at fret 12

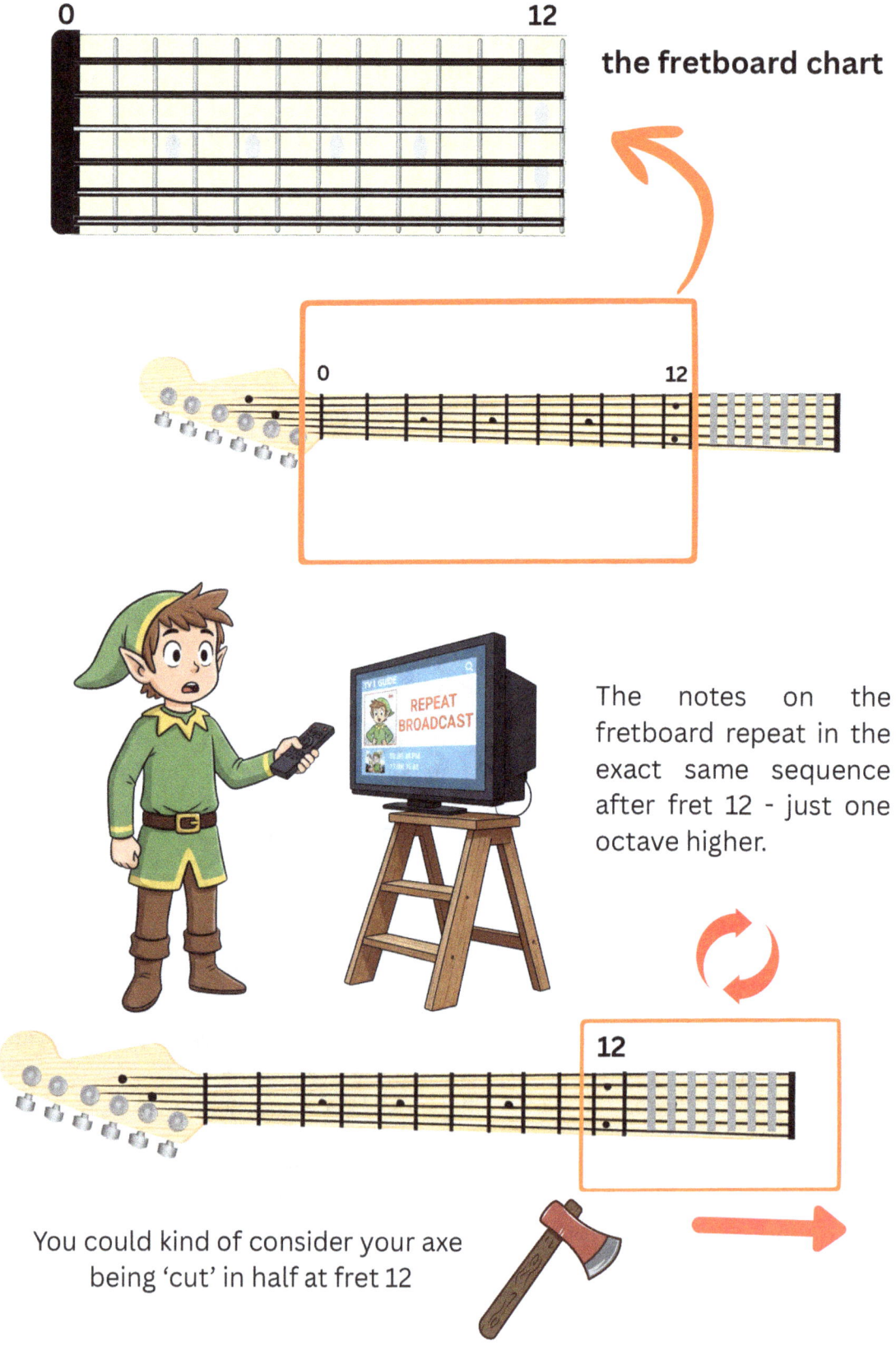

Just as the notes are "mirrored" on Frets 0-12, so the notes along the 1st and 6th strings are mirrored.

The difference between the notes along these strings is 2 octaves.

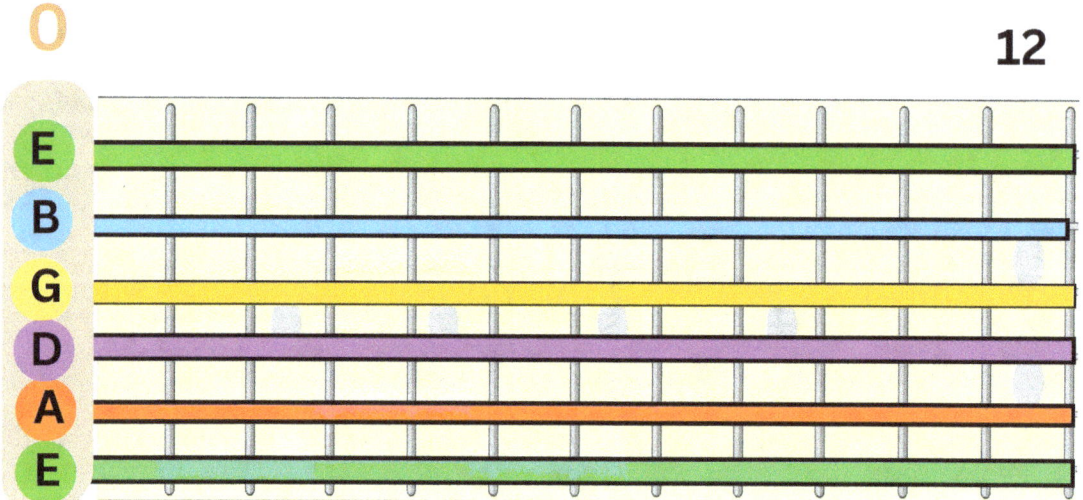

O = Open strings

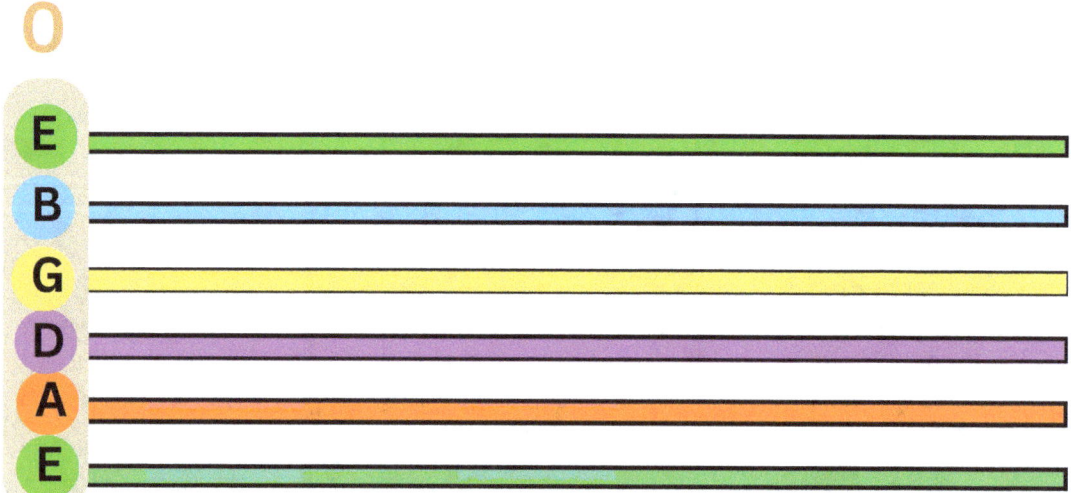

E

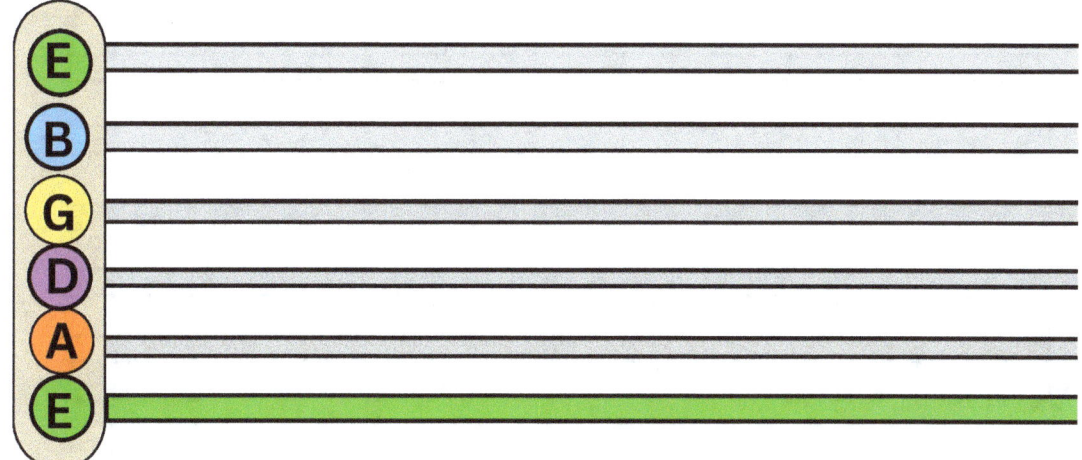

The 6th string (open)

6

A

The 5th string (open)

5

D

The 4th string (open)

4

The 3rd string (open)

3

The 2nd string (open)

2

E

The 1st string (open)

1

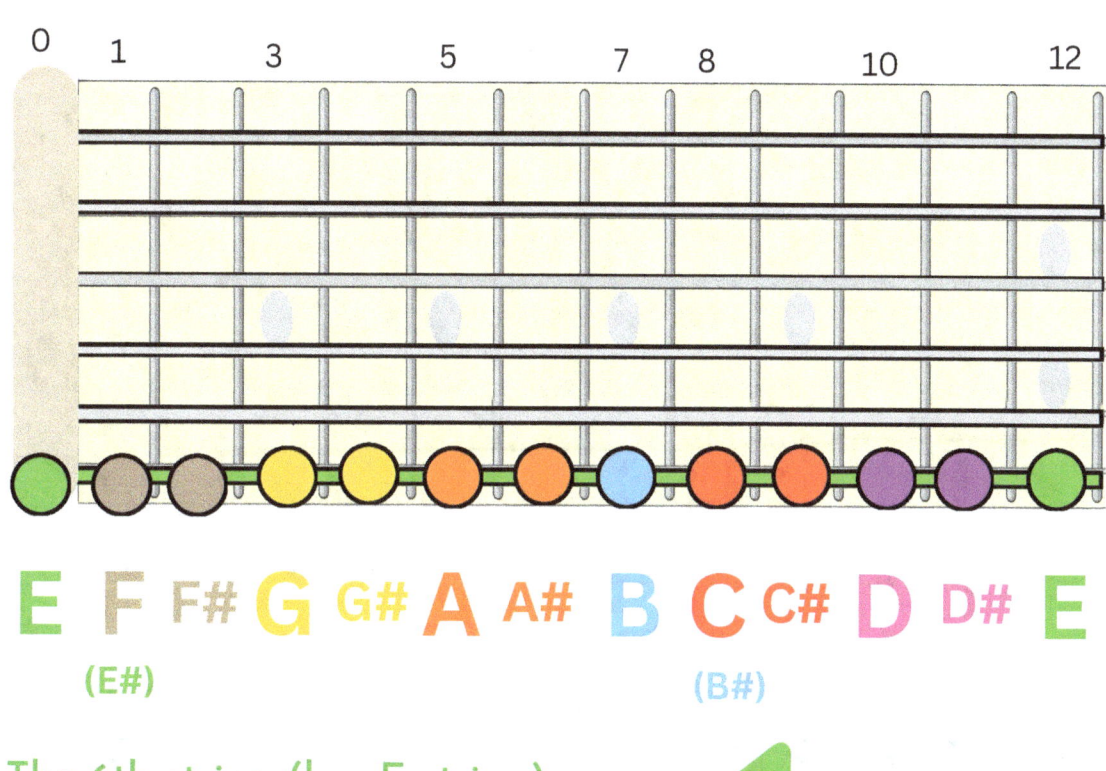

The 6th string (low E string)

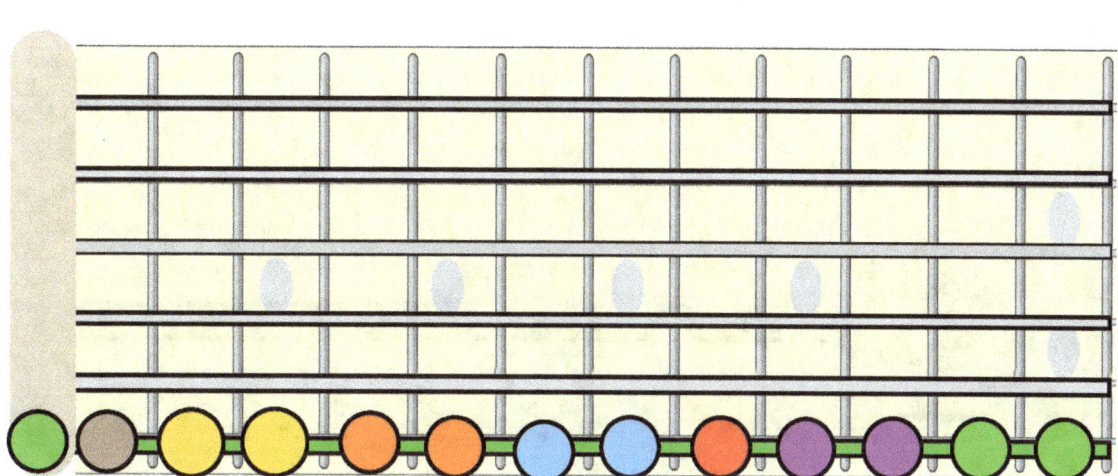

F

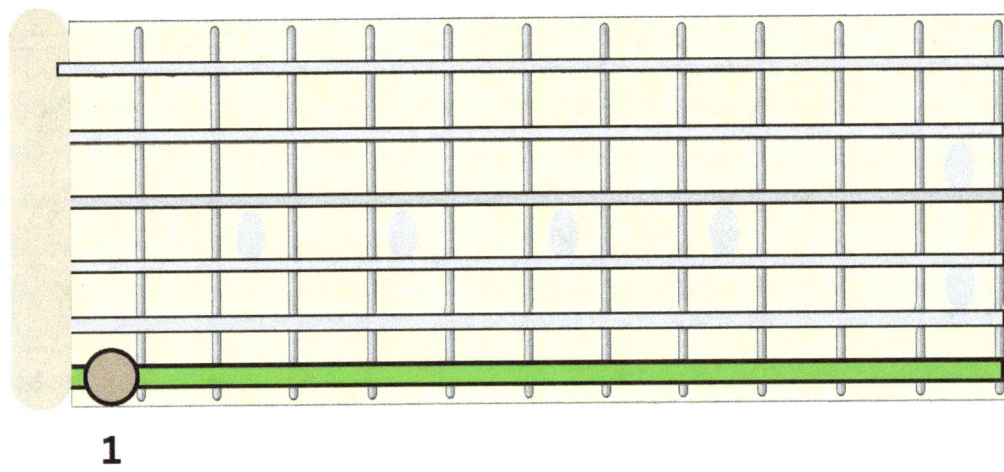

The 1st fret on the 6th string

Go to Fret 2 for F# and Fret 0 (Open string) for Fb

G

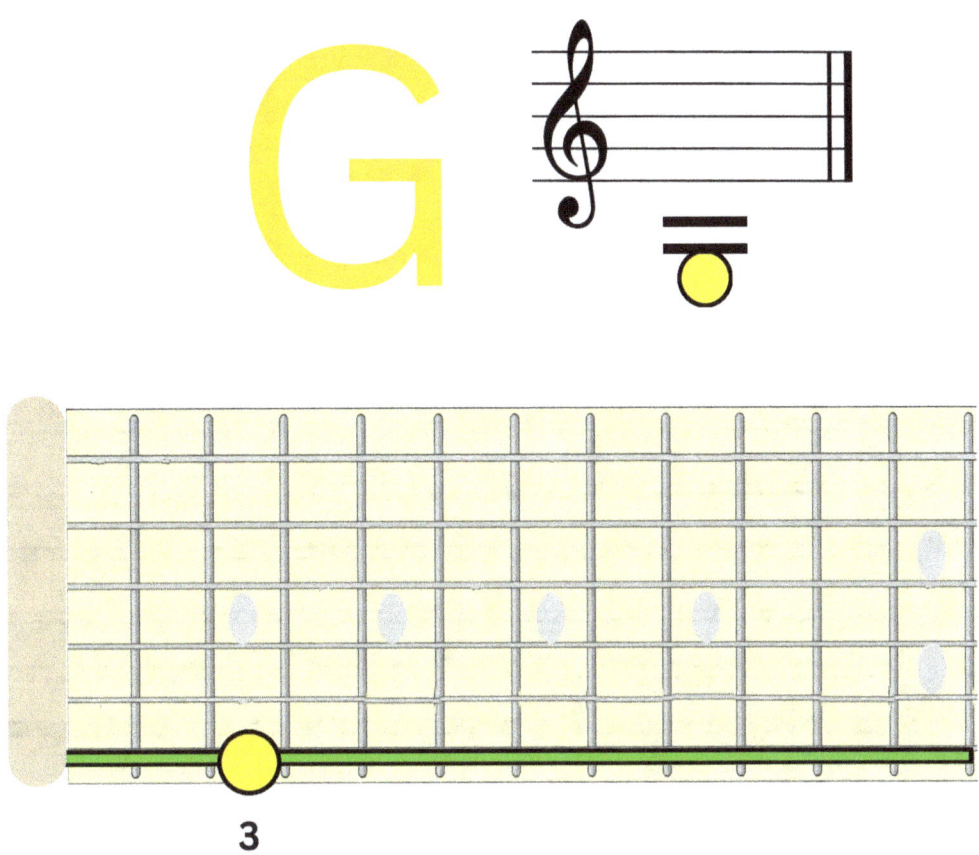

The 3rd fret on the 6th string

Go to Fret 4 for G# and Fret 2 for Gb

A

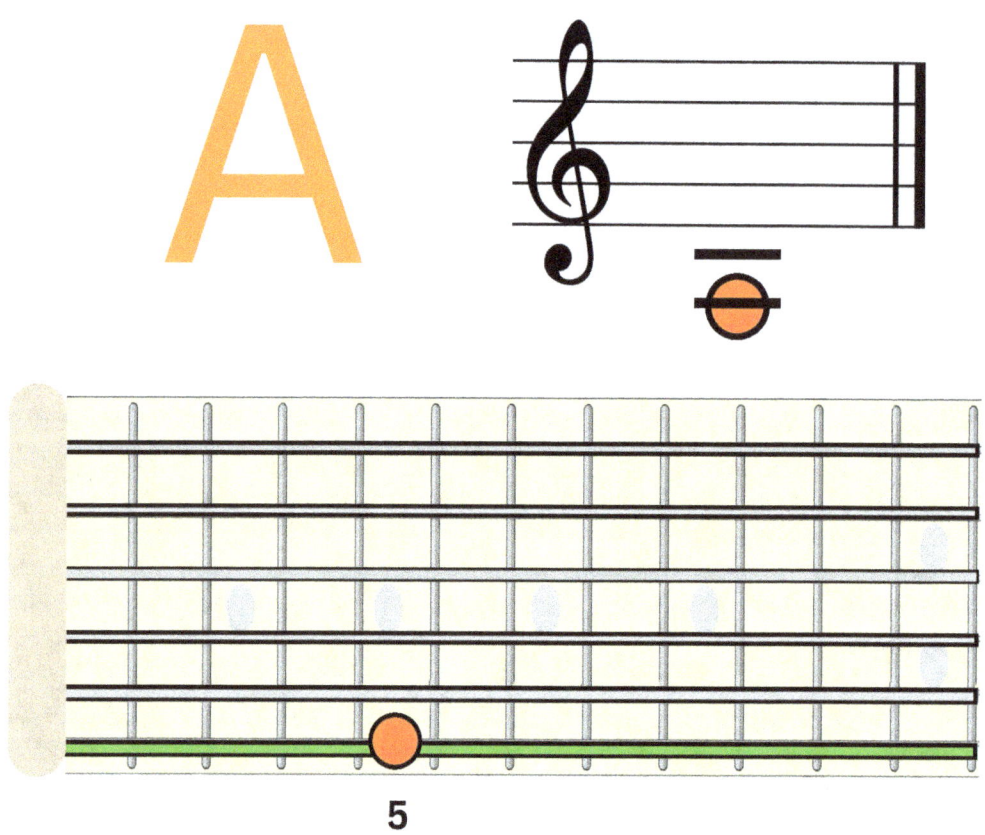

The 5th fret on the 6th string

Go to Fret 6 for A# and Fret 4 for Ab

B

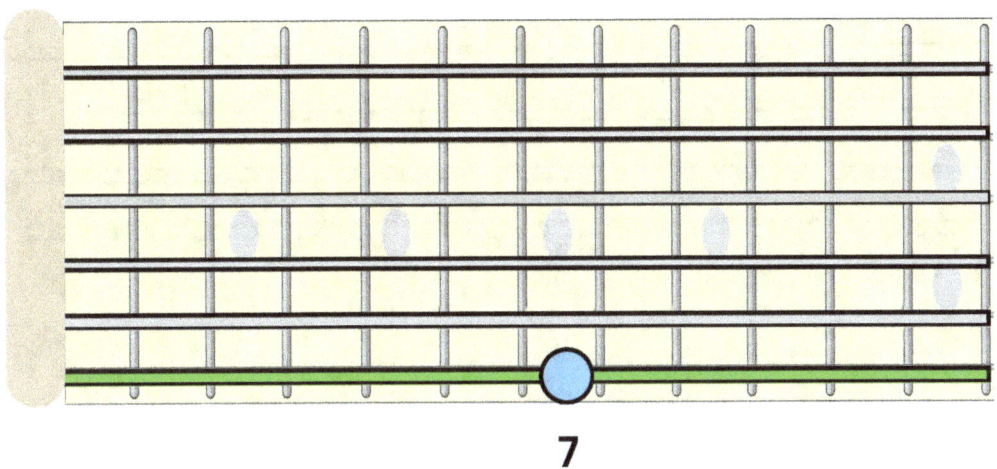

The 7th fret on the 6th string

Go to Fret 8 for B# and Fret 6 for Bb

C

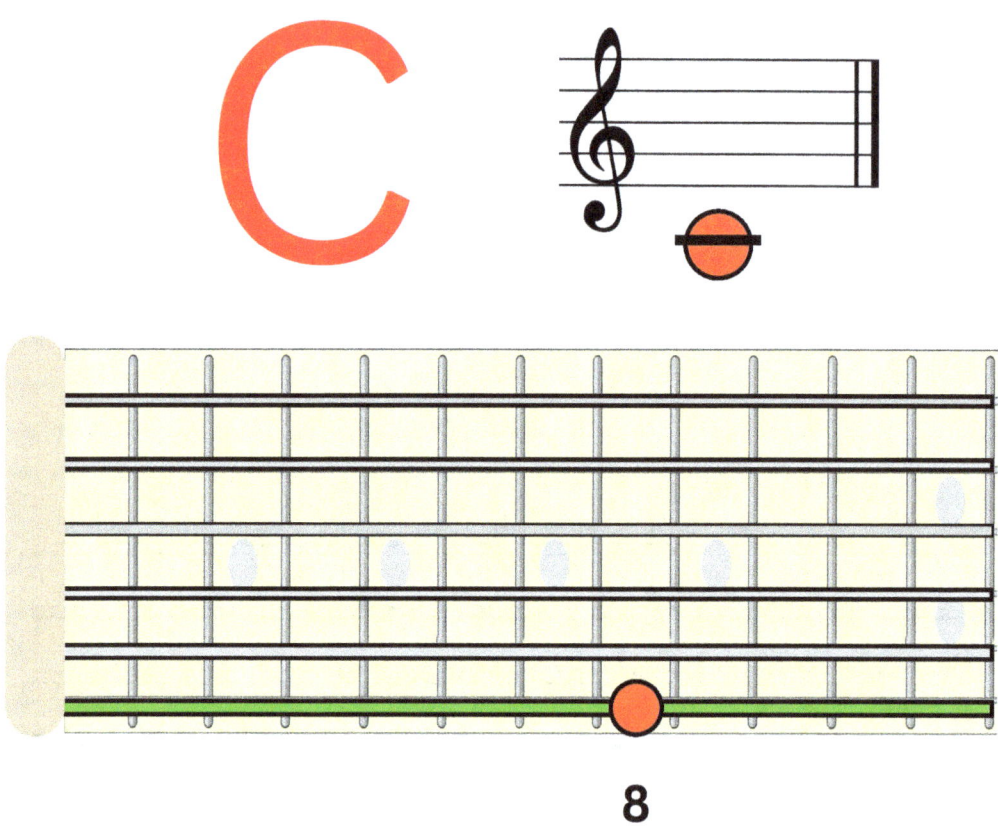

The 8th fret on the 6th string

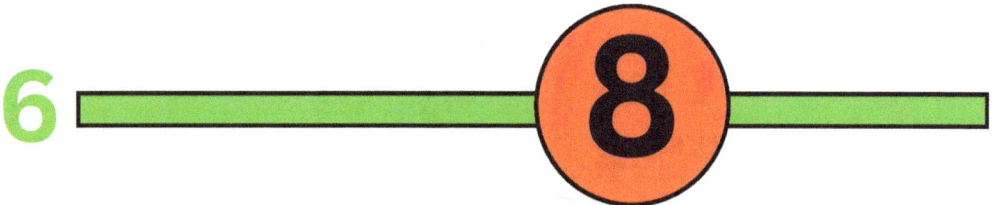

Go to Fret 9 for C# and Fret 7 for Cb

D

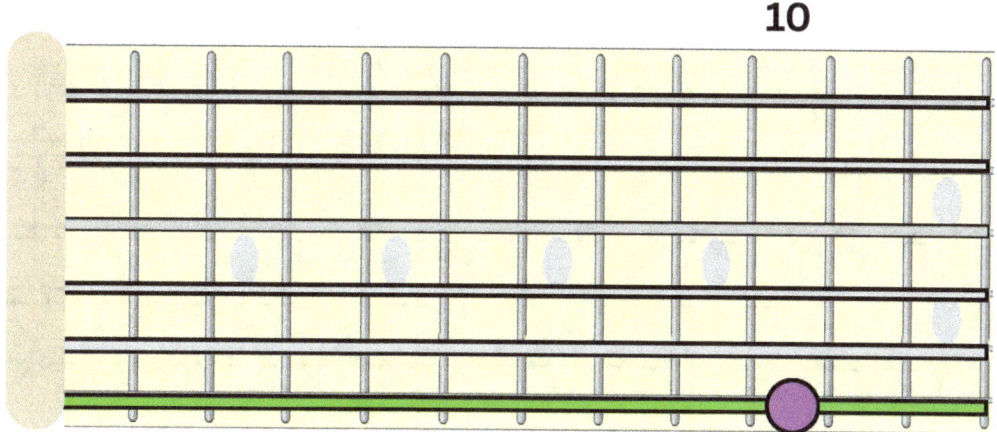

The 10th fret on the 6th string

Go to Fret 11 for D# and Fret 9 for Db

The 12th fret on the 6th string

Go to Fret 13 for E# and Fret 11 for Eb

A reminder that the fretboard notes on the 1st string (high E) follow the **same patten** as the 6th string (the low E string). The 1st are **higher in pitch by 2 octaves.**

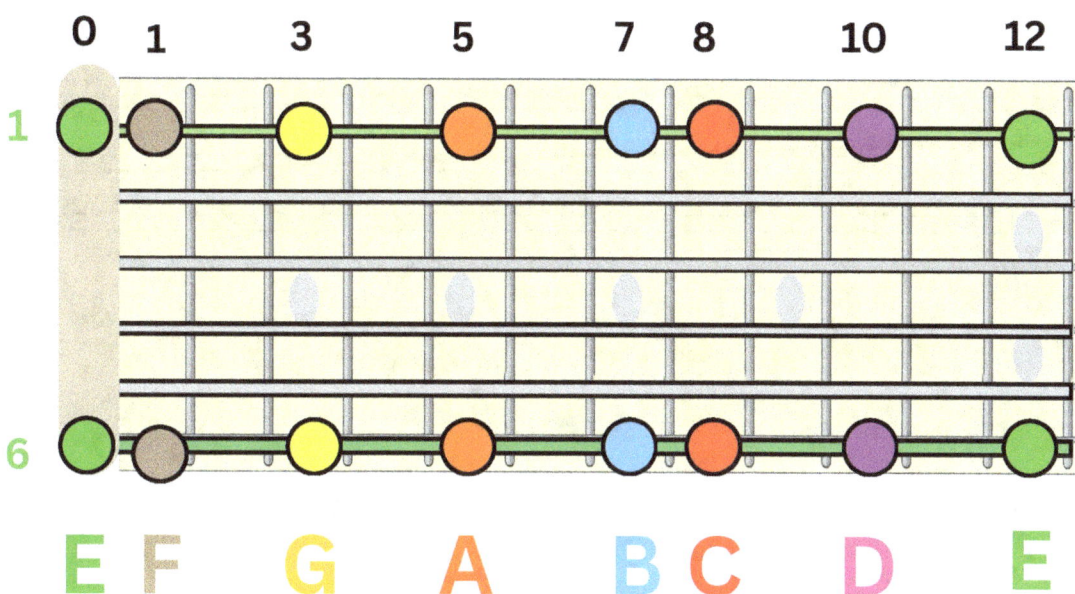

E F G A B C D E

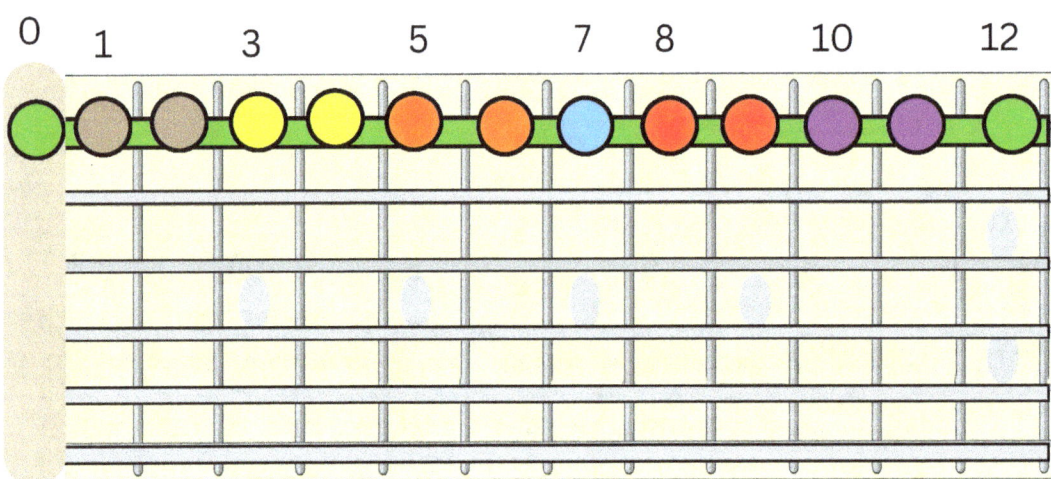

E F F# G G# A A# B C C# D D# E
(E#)   (B#)

The 1st string (high E string)

E F G♭ G A♭ A B♭ B C D♭ D E♭ E
(F♭)   (C♭)

E

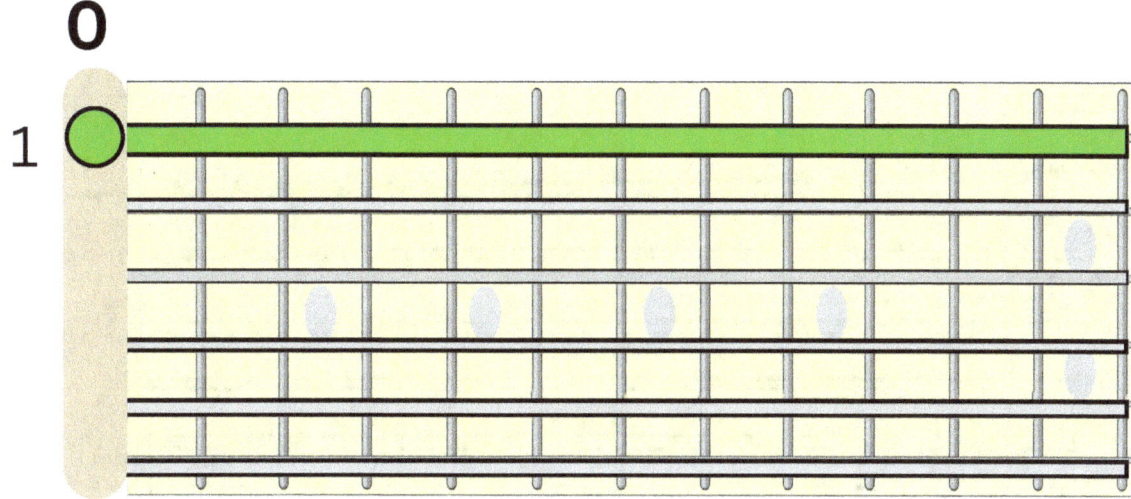

The open 1st string

Go to Fret 1 for E#

F

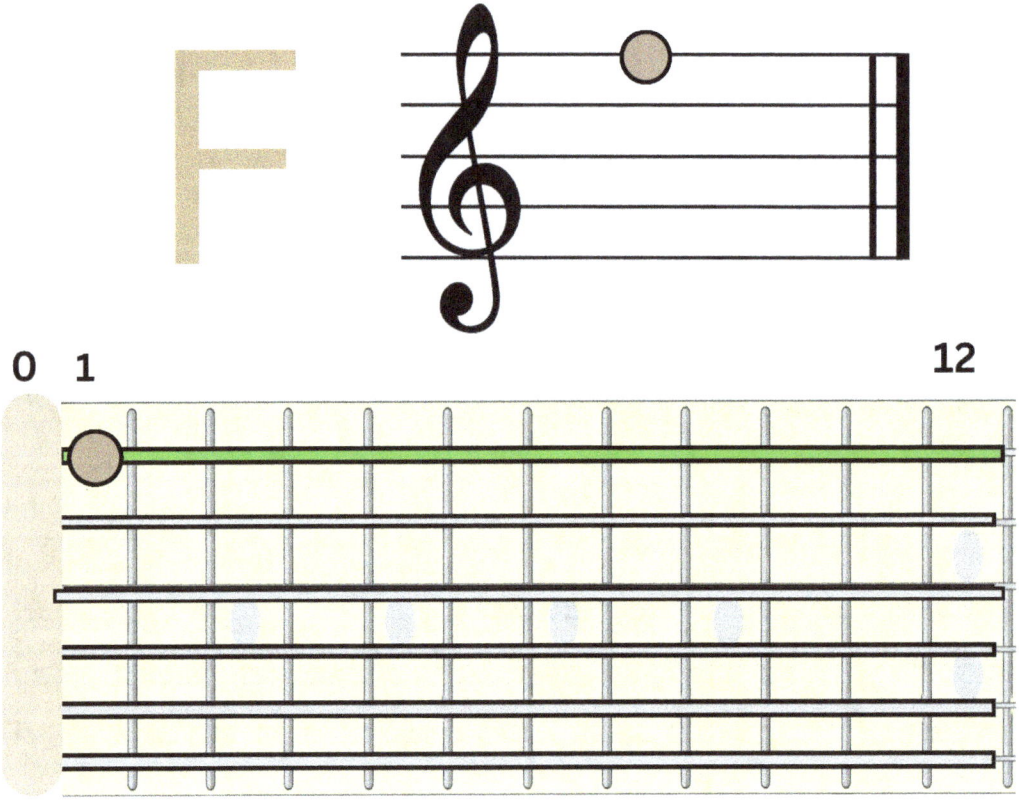

The 1st fret on the 1st string

Go to Fret 2 for F# and Fret 0 (open) for Fb

G

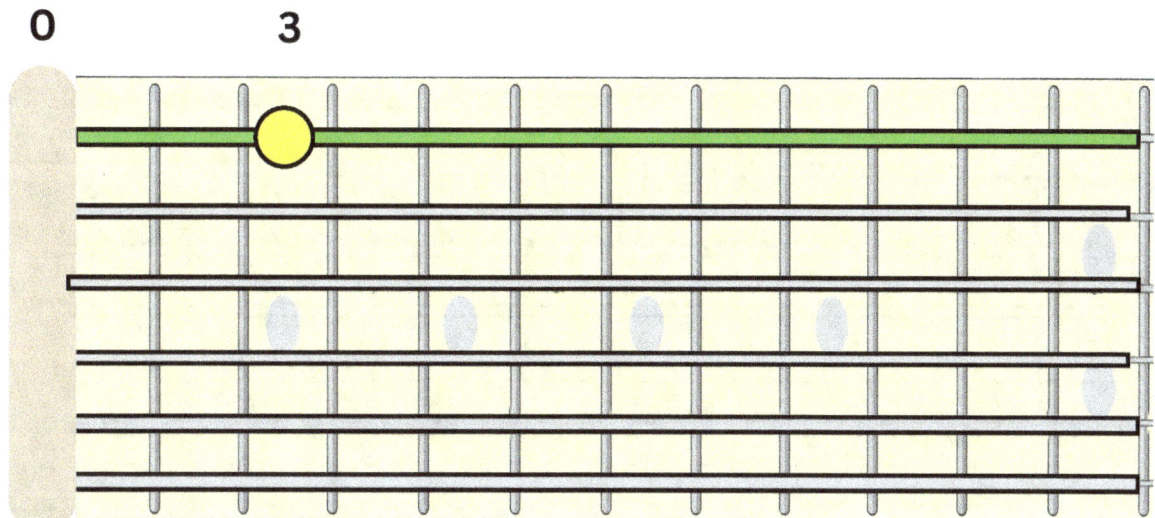

The 3rd fret on the 1st string

Go to Fret 4 for G# and Fret 2 for Gb

A

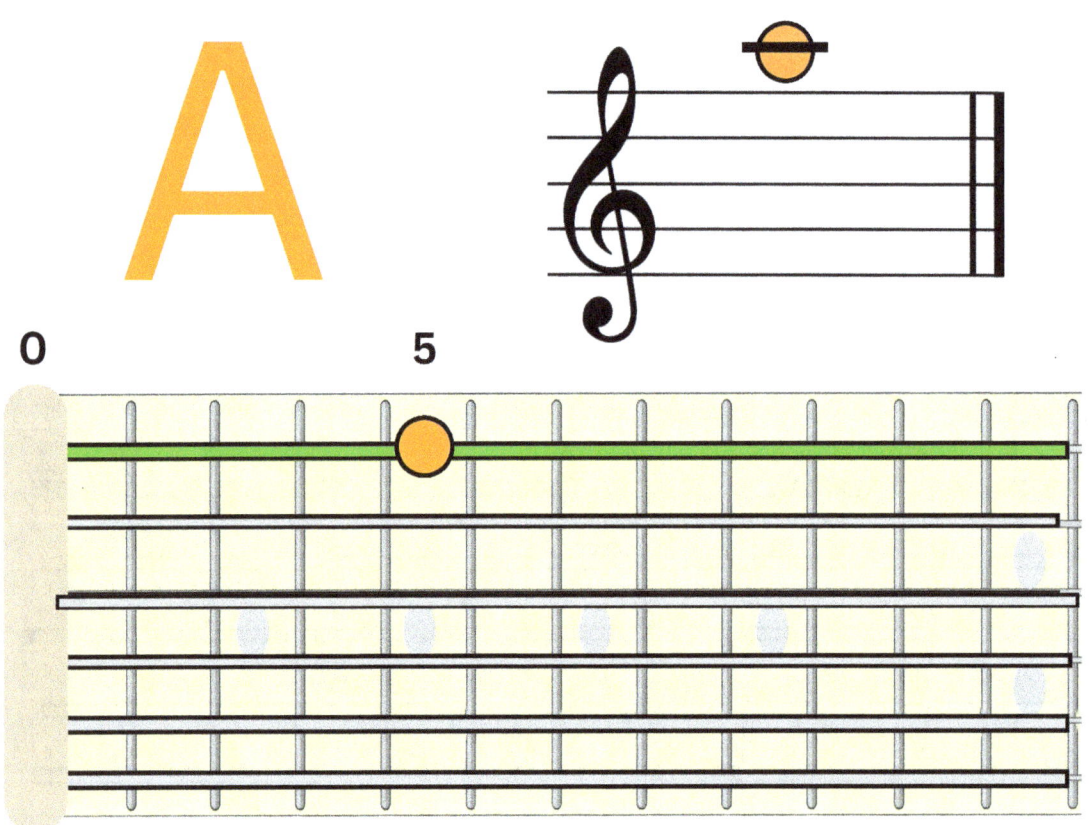

The 5th fret on the 1st string

Go to Fret 6 for A# and Fret 4 for Ab

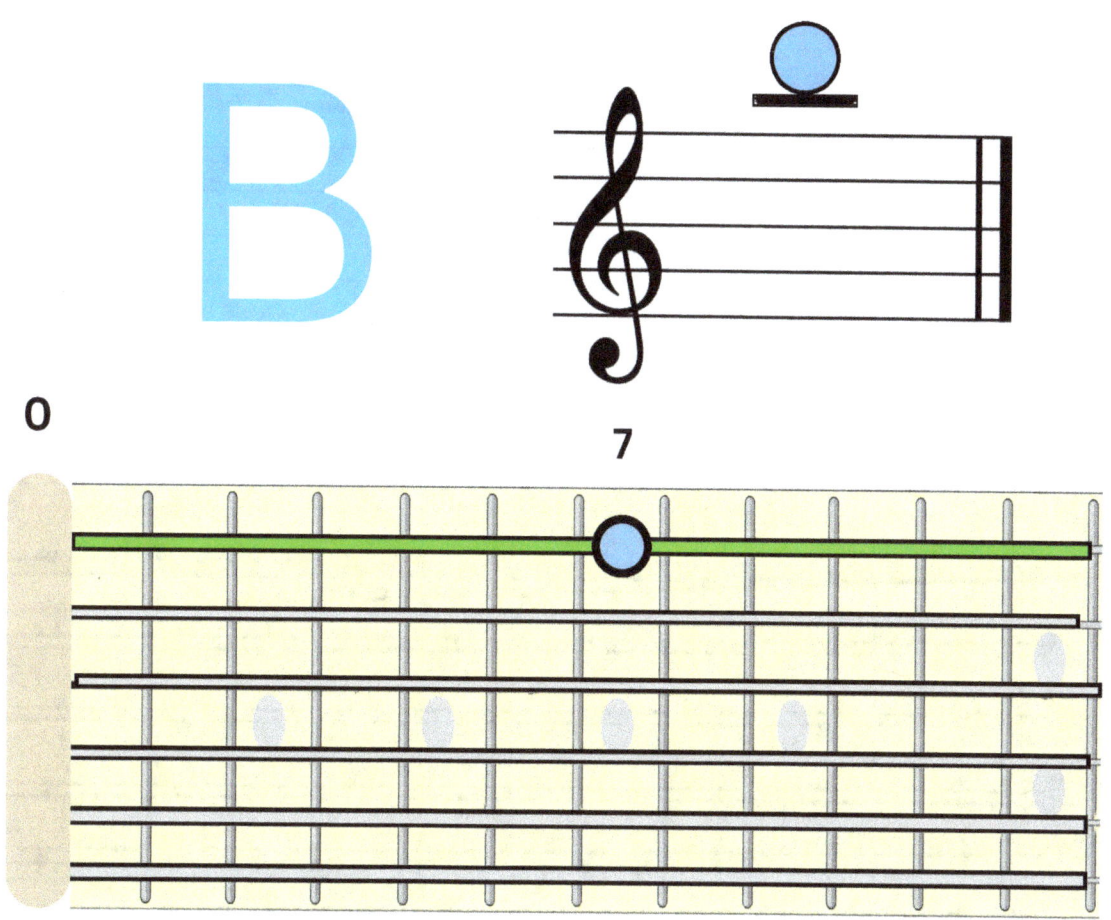

The 7th fret on the 1st string

Go to Fret 8 for B# and Fret 6 for Bb

C

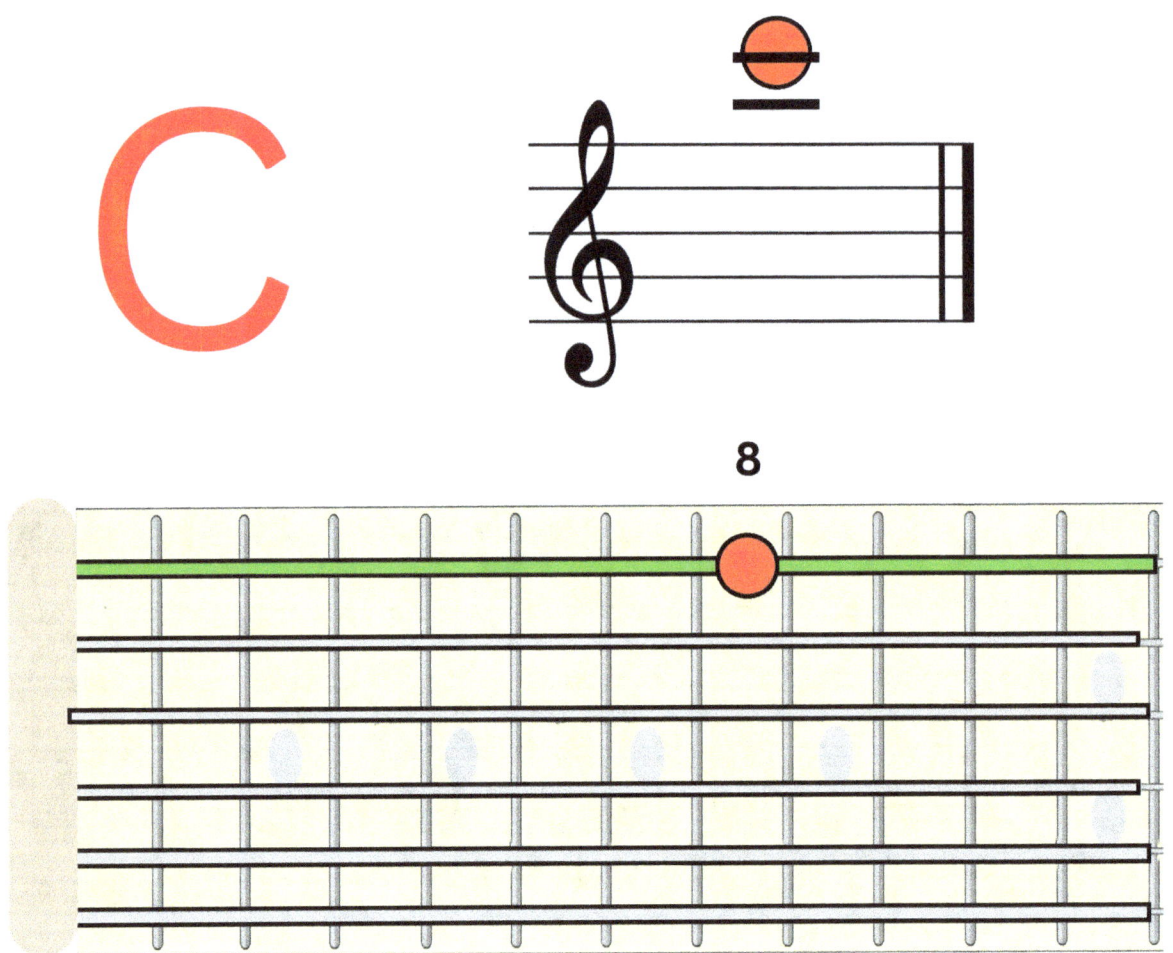

The 8th fret on the 1st string

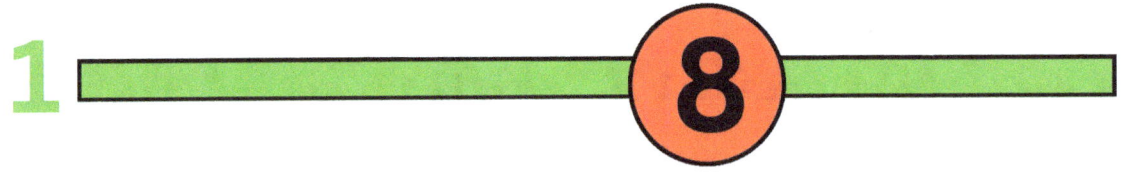

Go to Fret 9 for C# and Fret 7 for Cb

D

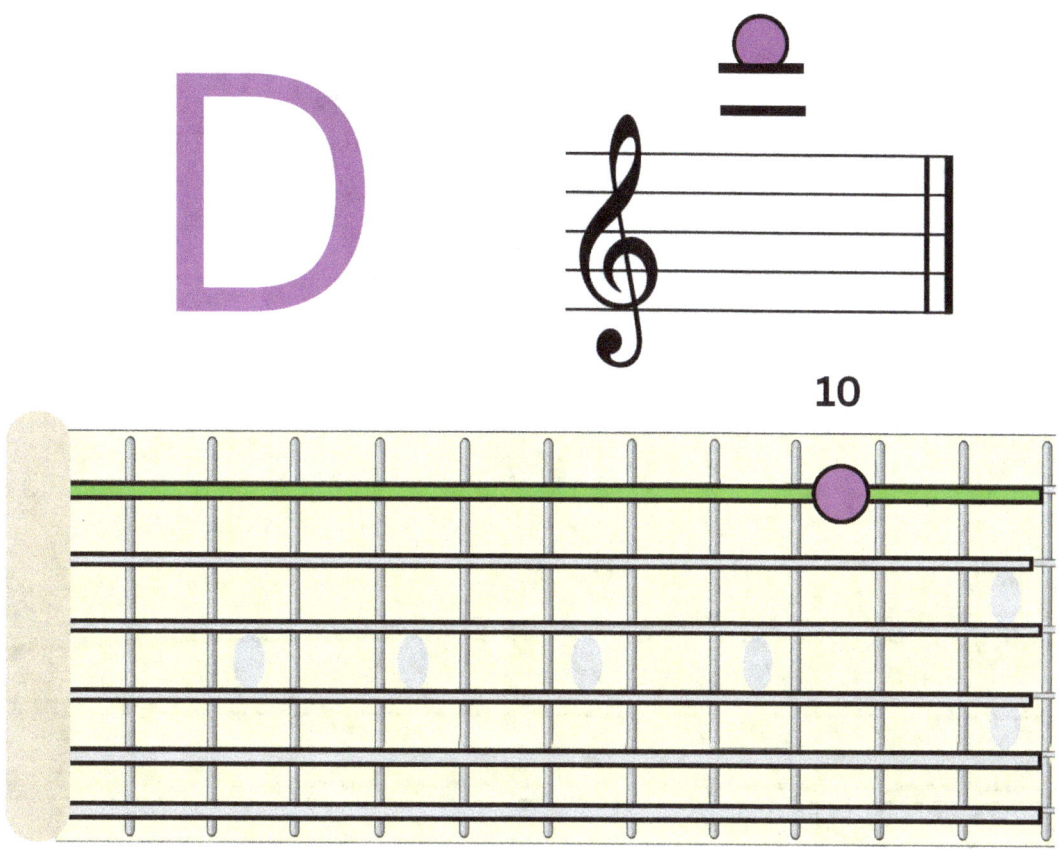

The 10th fret on the 1st string

Go to Fret 11 for D# and Fret 9 for Db

The 12th fret on the 1st string

Go to Fret 13 for E# and Fret 11 for Eb

Notes on the A string - the 5th string

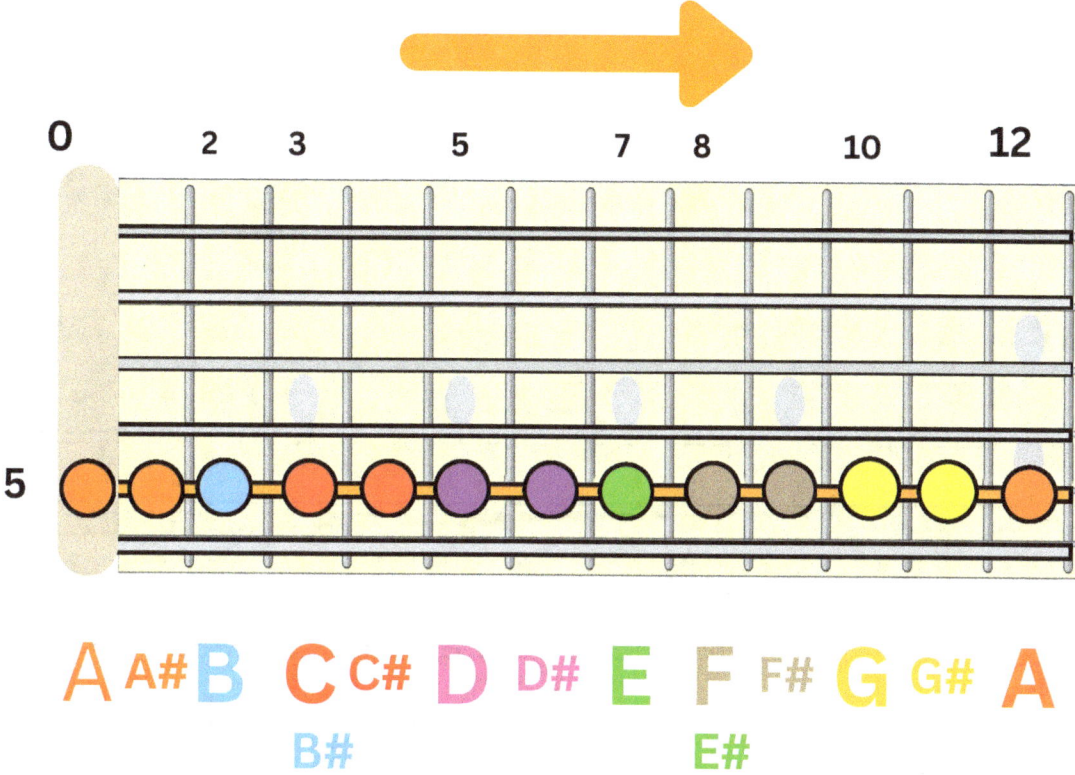

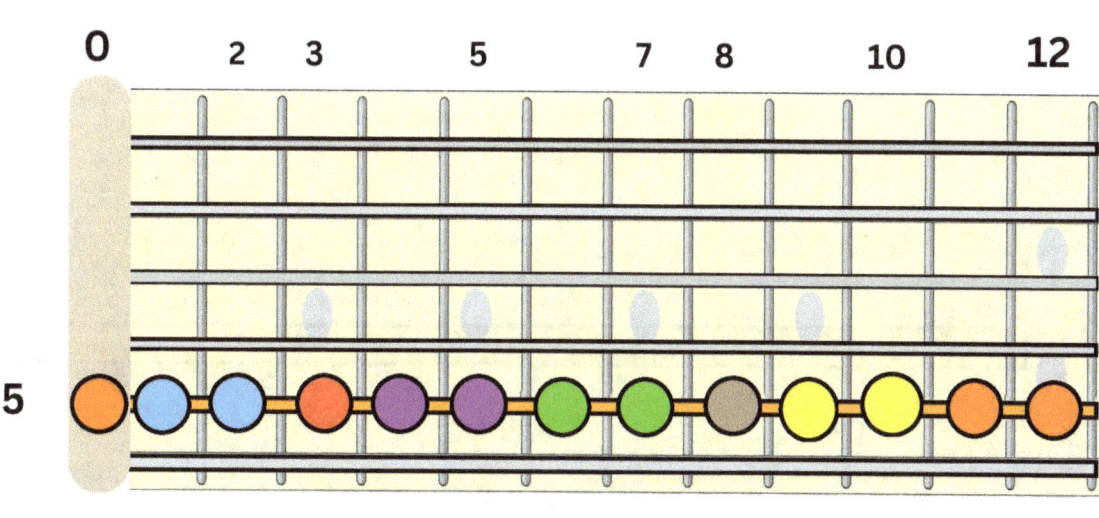

A

The open 5th string

5

Go to Fret 1 for A#

B

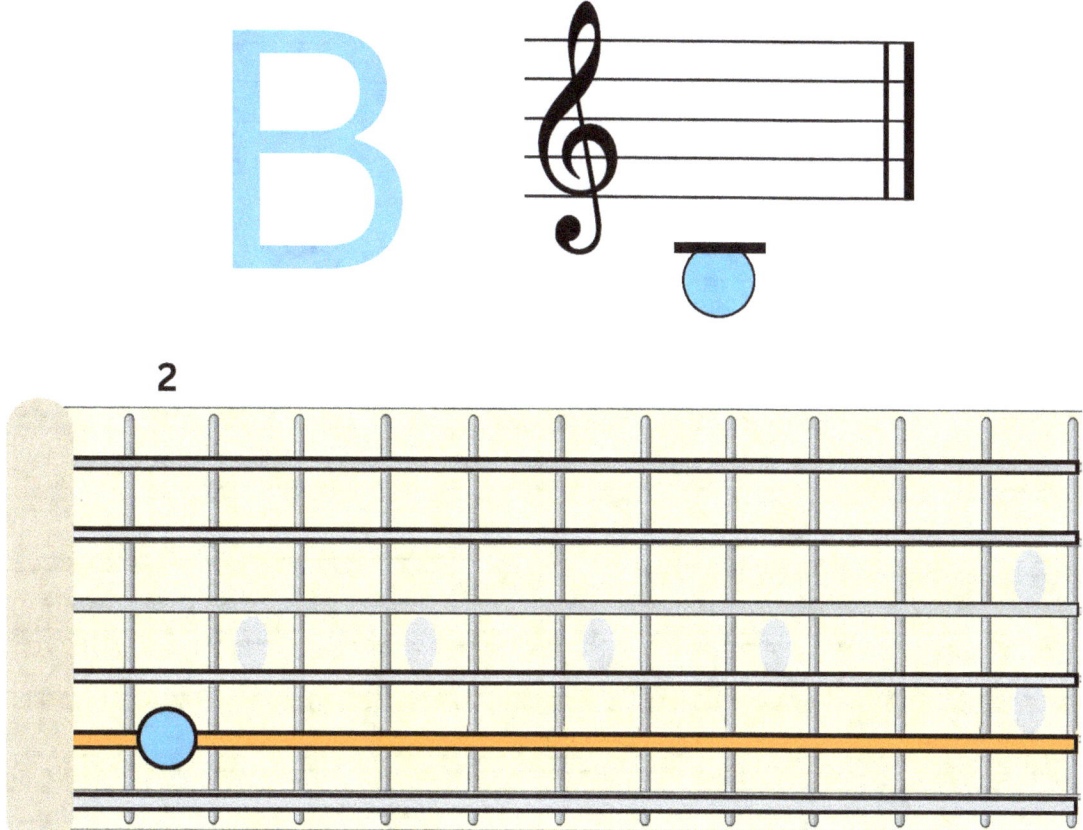

The 2nd fret on the 5th string

Go to Fret 3 for B# and Fret 1 for Bb

The 3rd fret on the 5th string

Go to Fret 4 for C# and Fret 2 for C♭

D

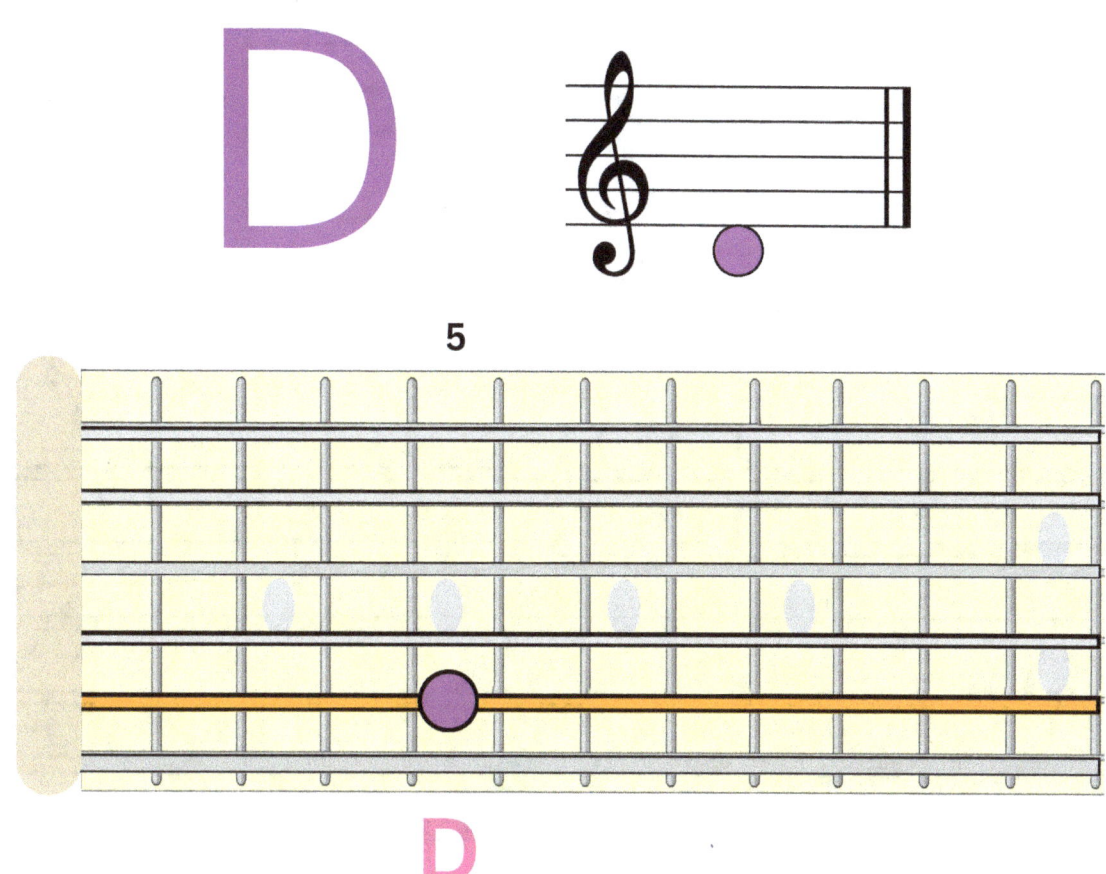

The 5th fret on the 5th string

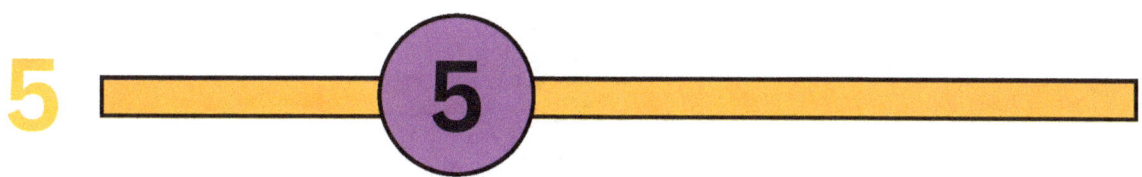

Go to Fret 6 for D# and Fret 4 for Db

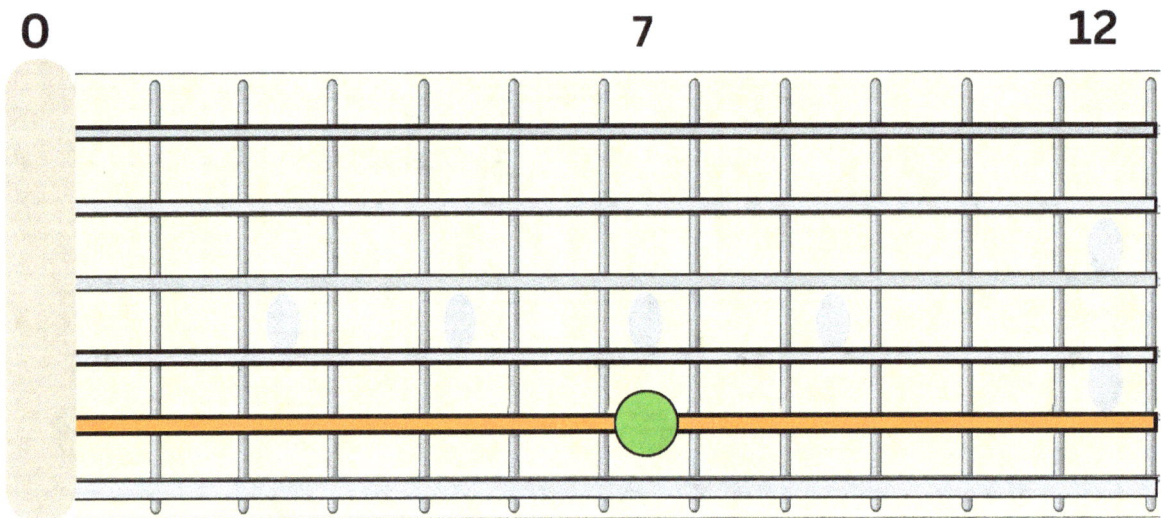

The 7th fret on the 5th string

Go to Fret 8 for E# and Fret 6 for Eb

F

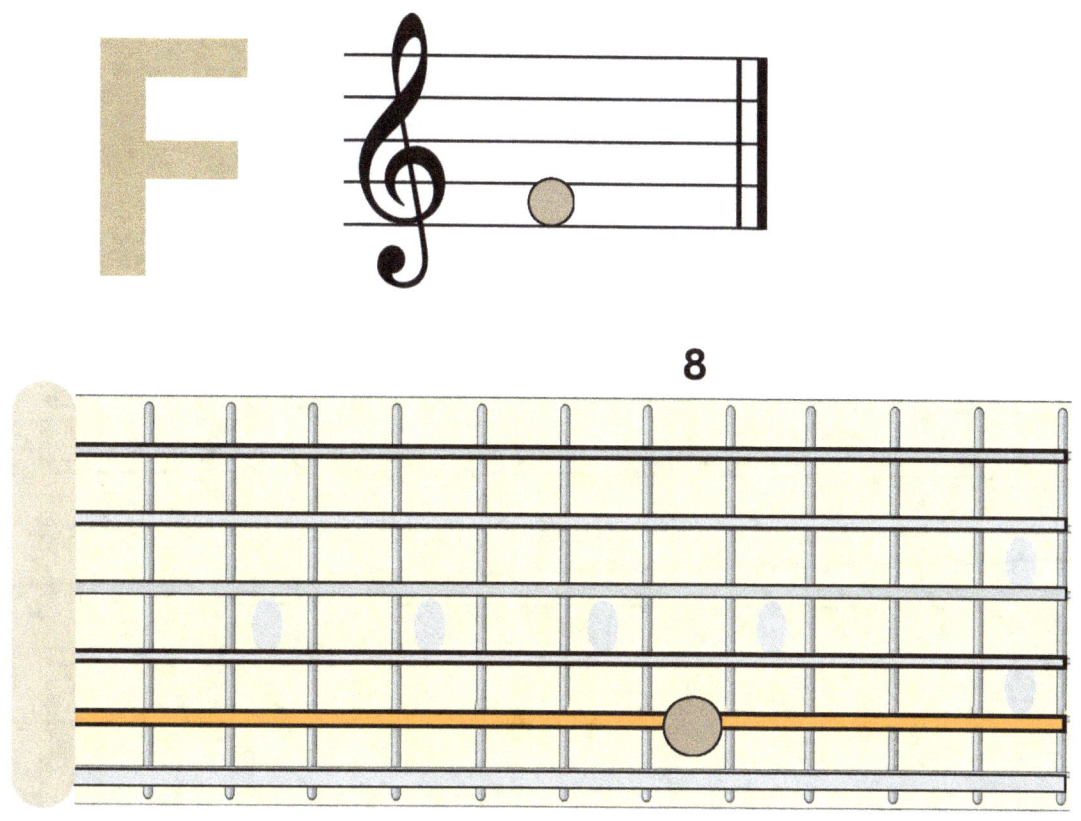

The 8th fret on the 5th string

Go to Fret 9 for F# and Fret 7 for Fb

G

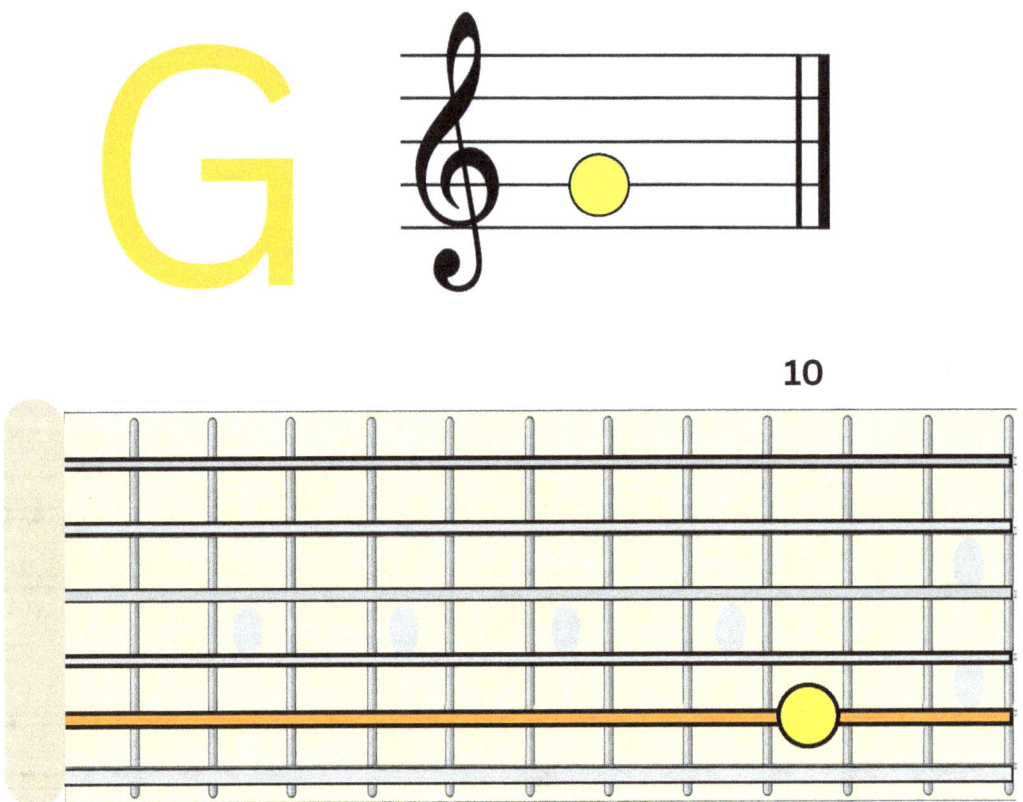

The 10th fret on the 5th string

Go to Fret 11 for G# and Fret 9 for Gb

A

The 12th fret on the 5th string

Go to Fret 13 for A# and Fret 11 for Ab

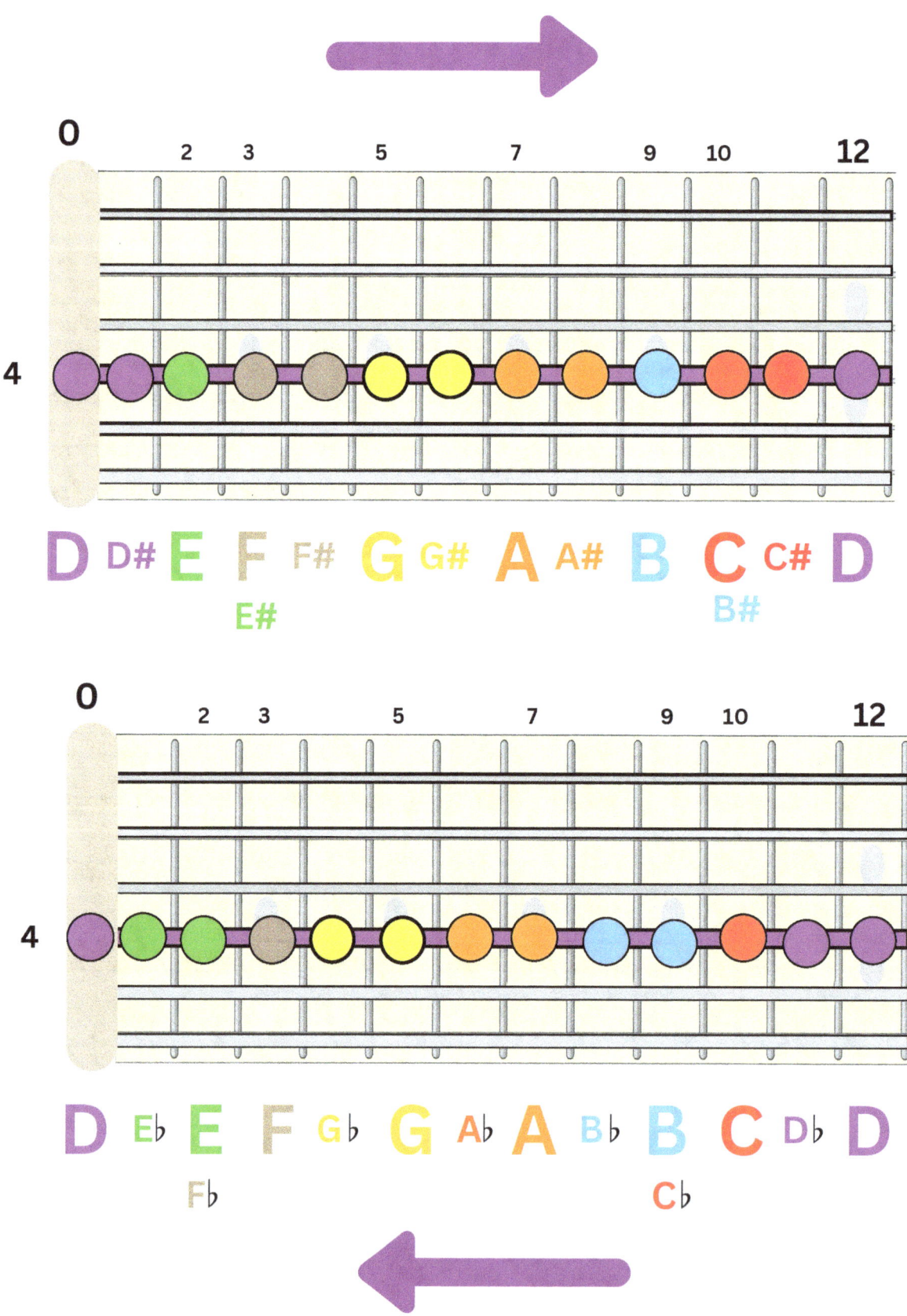

D

The open 4th string

4

Go to Fret 1 for D#

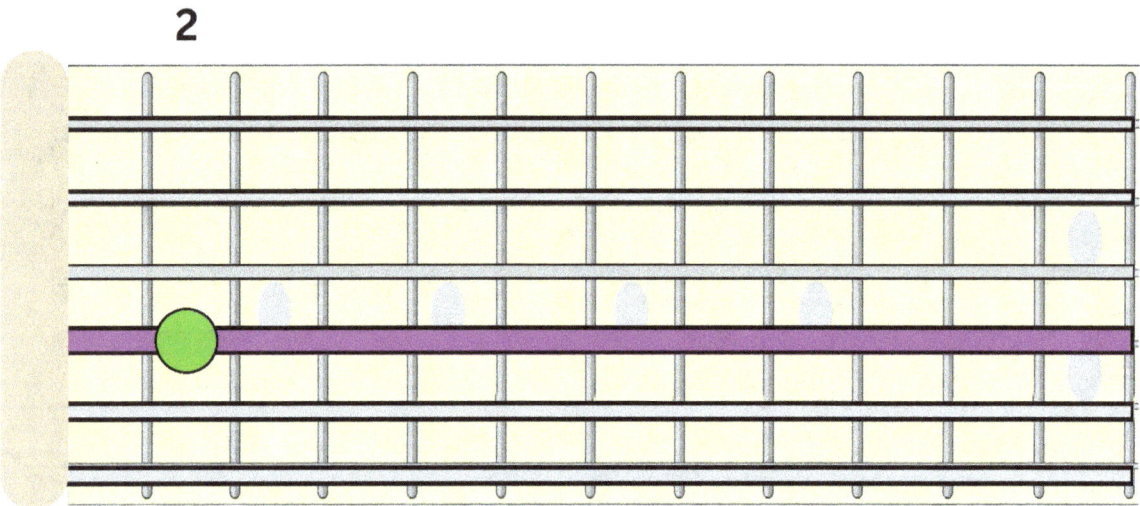

The 2nd fret on the 4th string

Go to Fret 3 for E# and Fret 1 for Eb

F

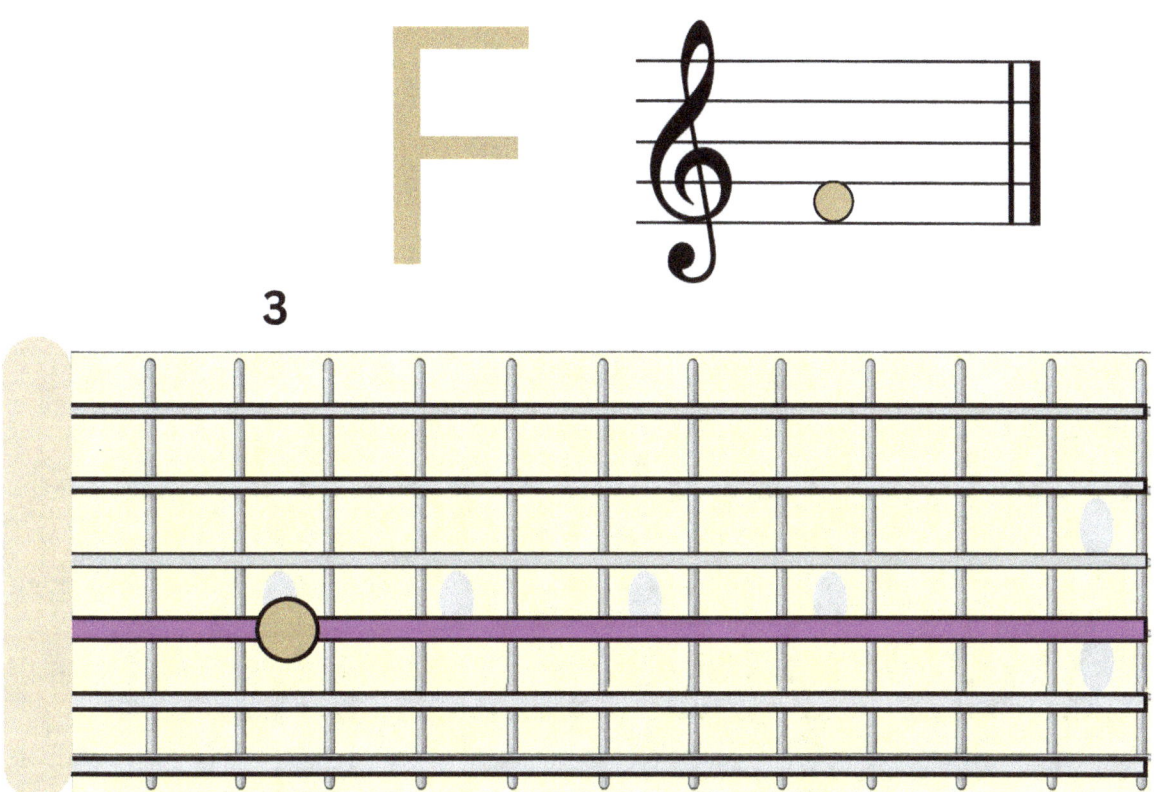

The 3rd fret on the 4th string

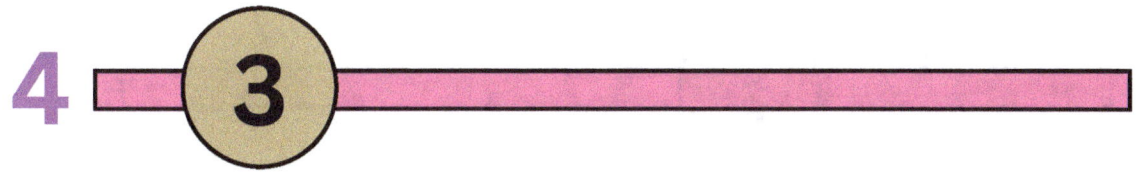

Go to Fret 4 for F# and Fret 2 for Fb

G

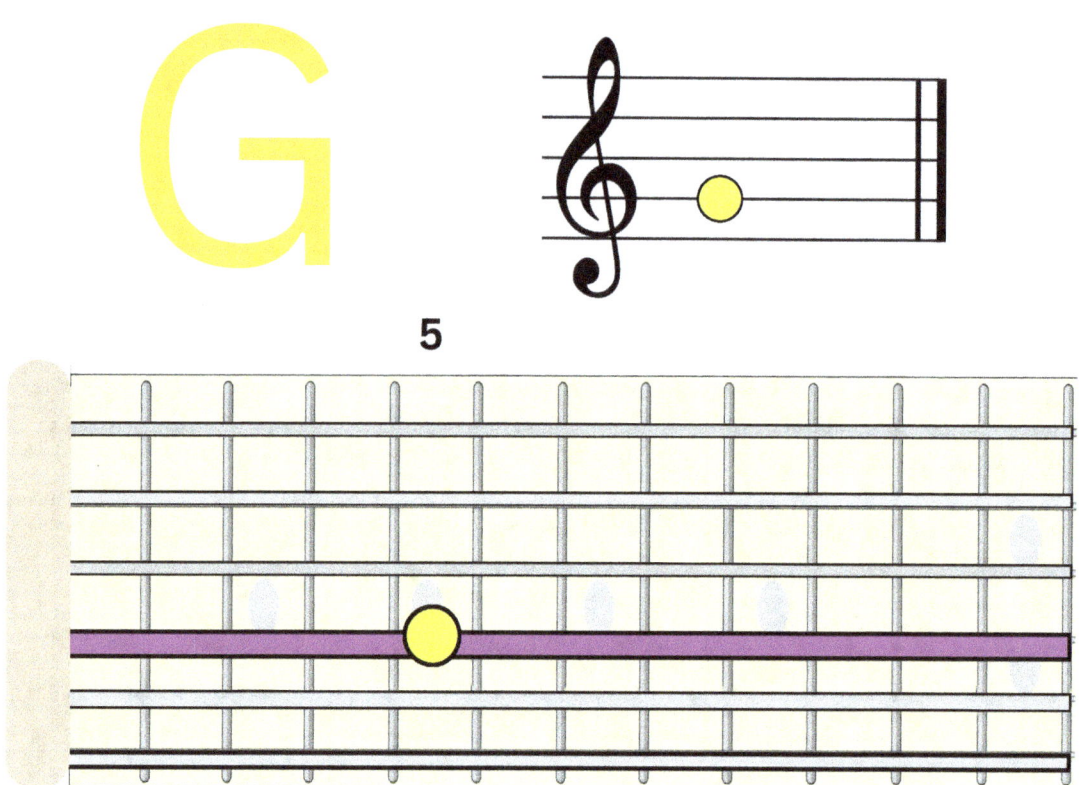

The 5th fret on the 4th string

Go to Fret 6 for G# and Fret 4 for Gb

A

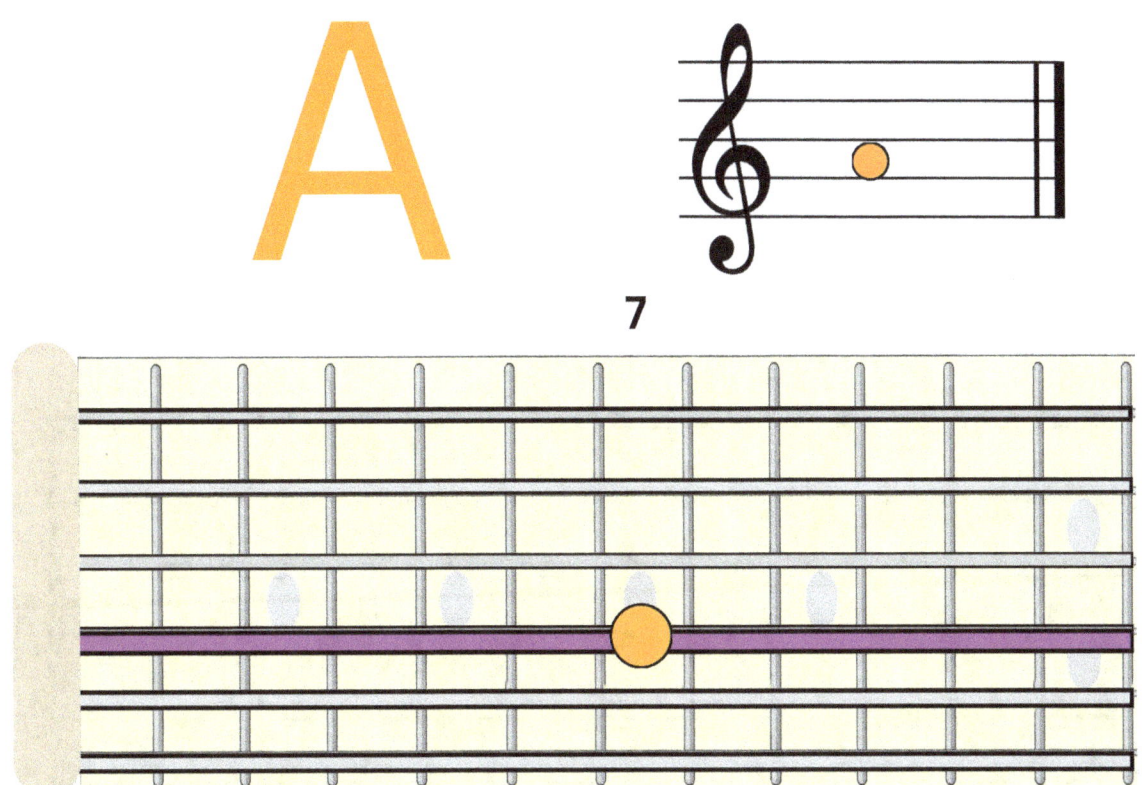

The 7th fret on the 4th string

Go to Fret 8 for A# and Fret 6 for Ab

B

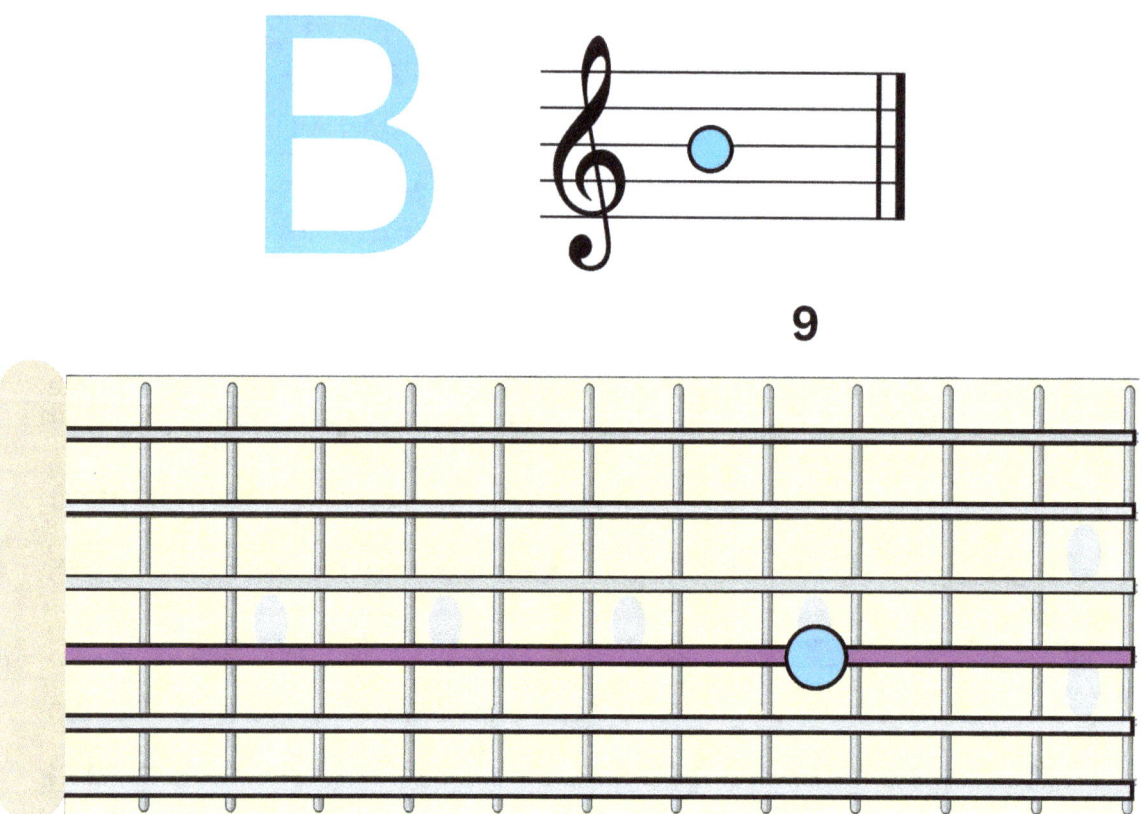

The 9th fret on the 4th string

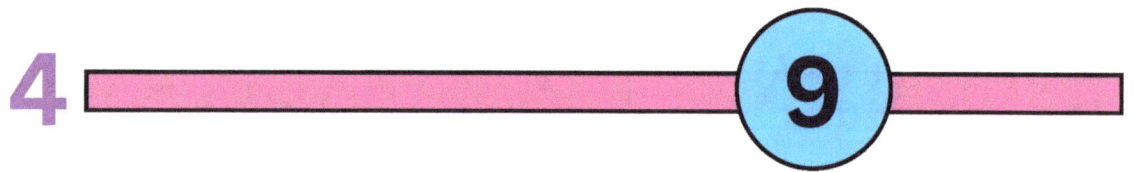

Go to Fret 10 for B# and Fret 8 for Bb

C

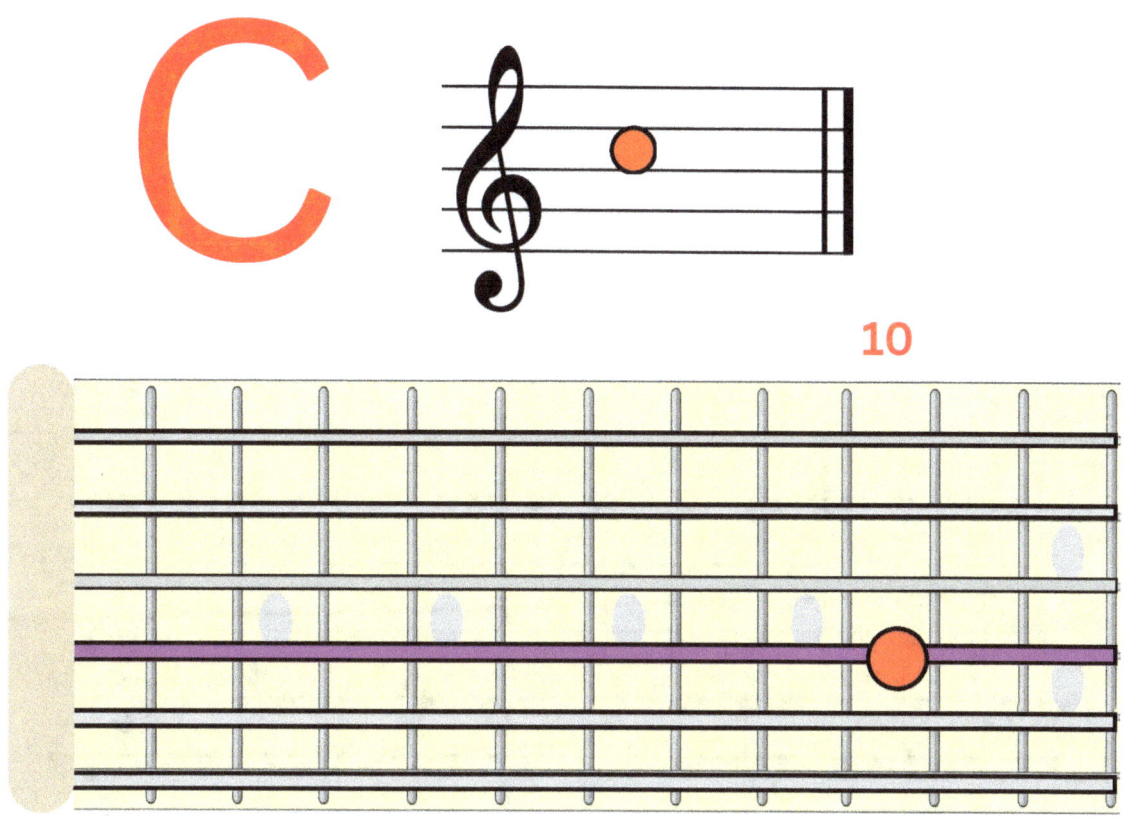

The 10th fret on the 4th string

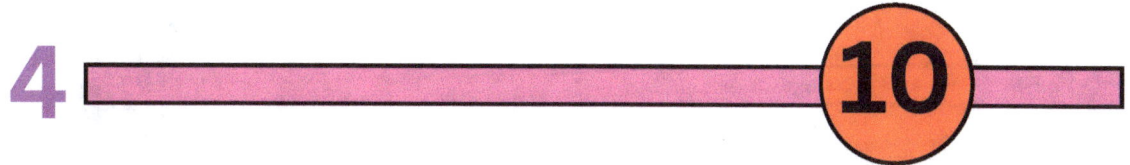

Go to Fret 11 for C# and Fret 9 for Cb

D

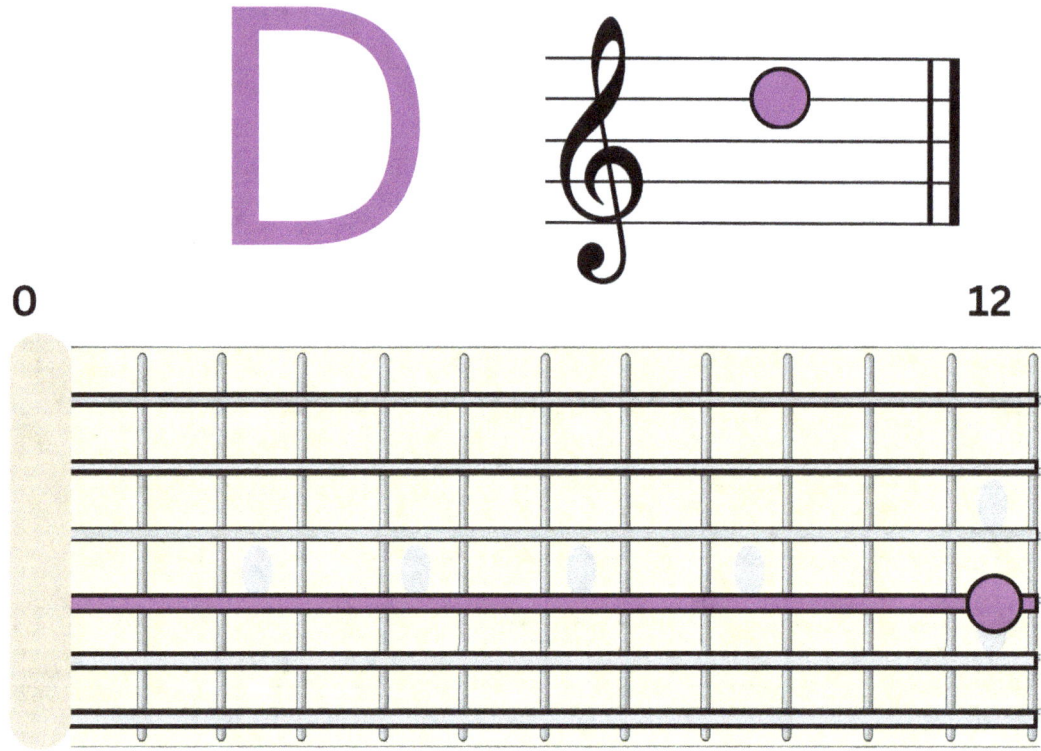

The 12th fret on the 4th string

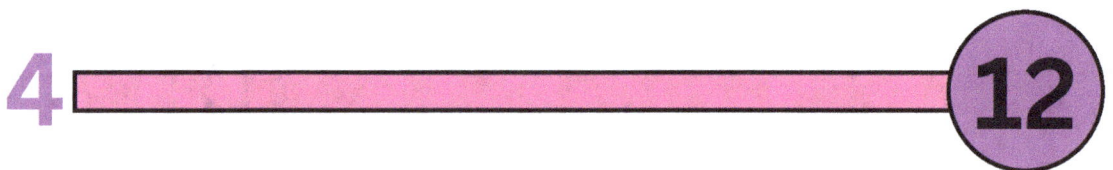

Go to Fret 13 for D# and Fret 11 for Db

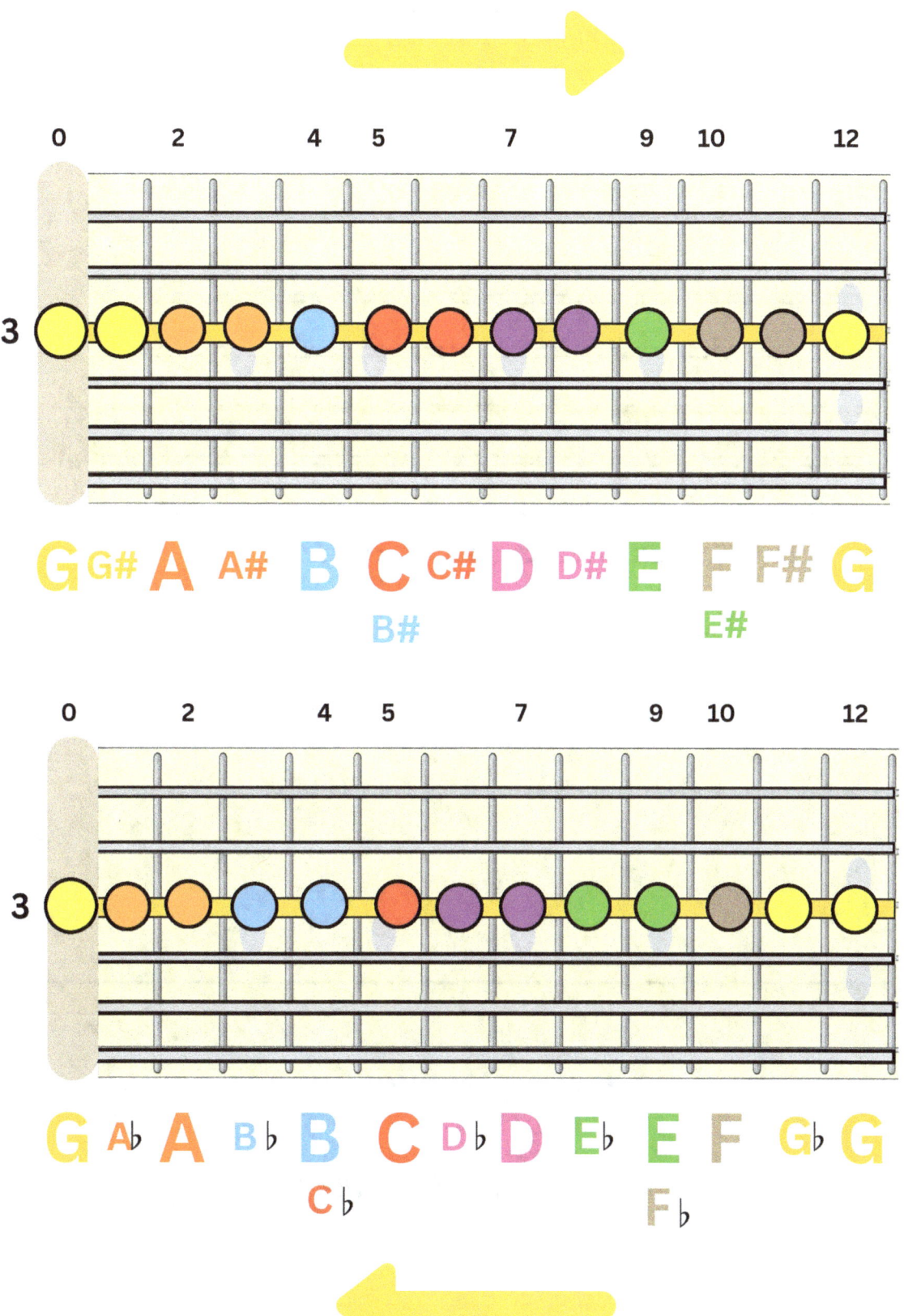

G

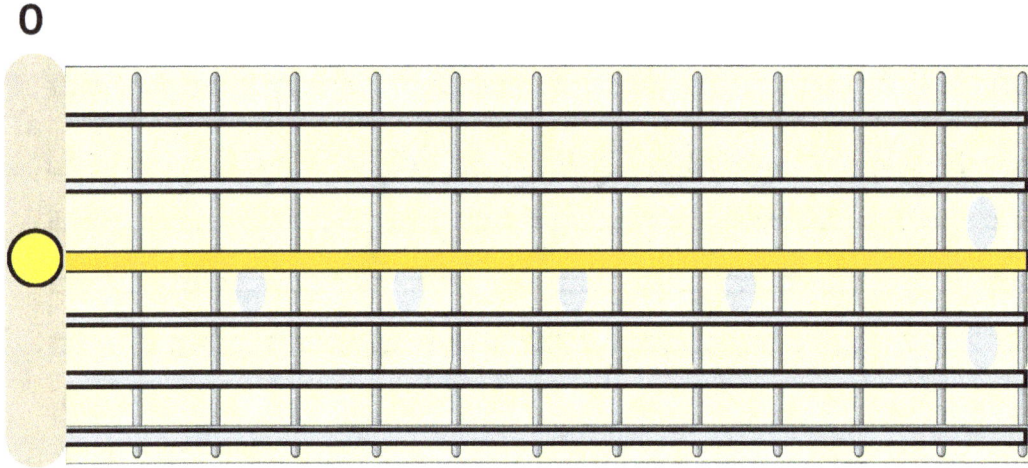

The open 3rd string

3

Go to Fret 1 for G#

A

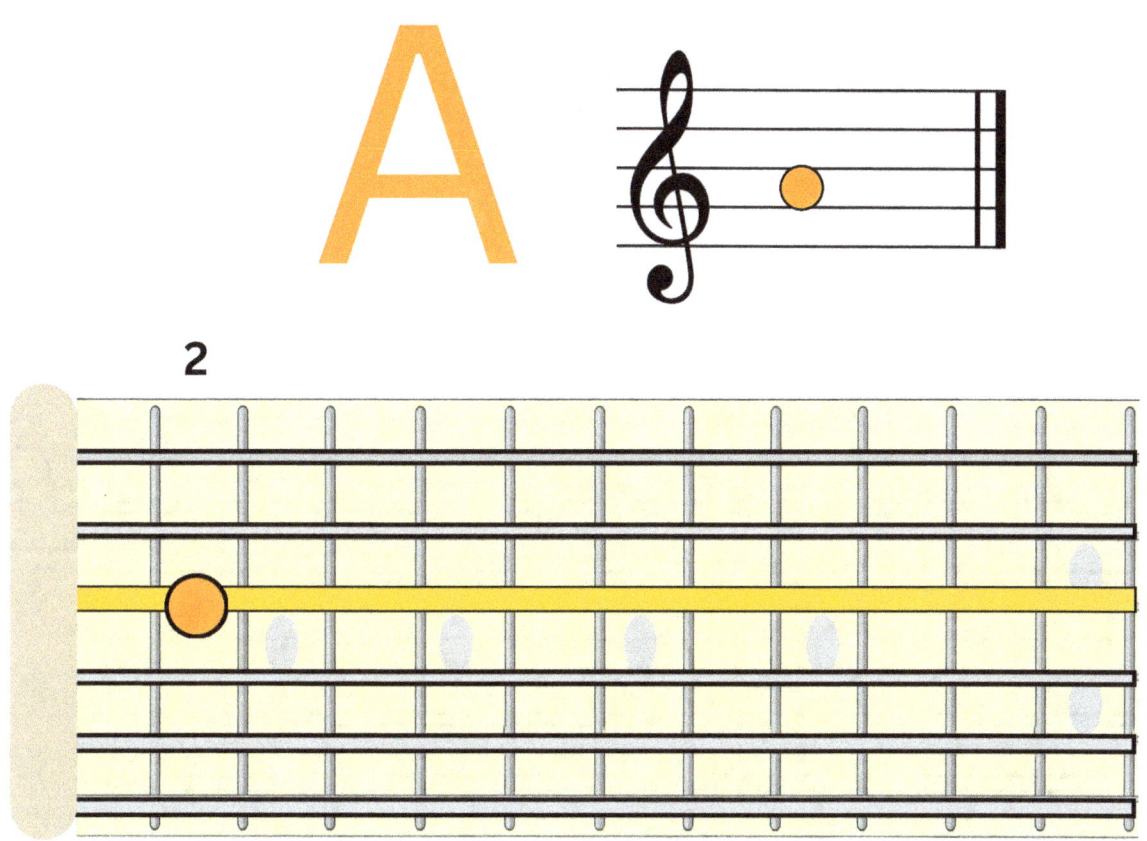

The 2nd fret on the 3rd string

Go to Fret 3 for A# and Fret 1 for Ab

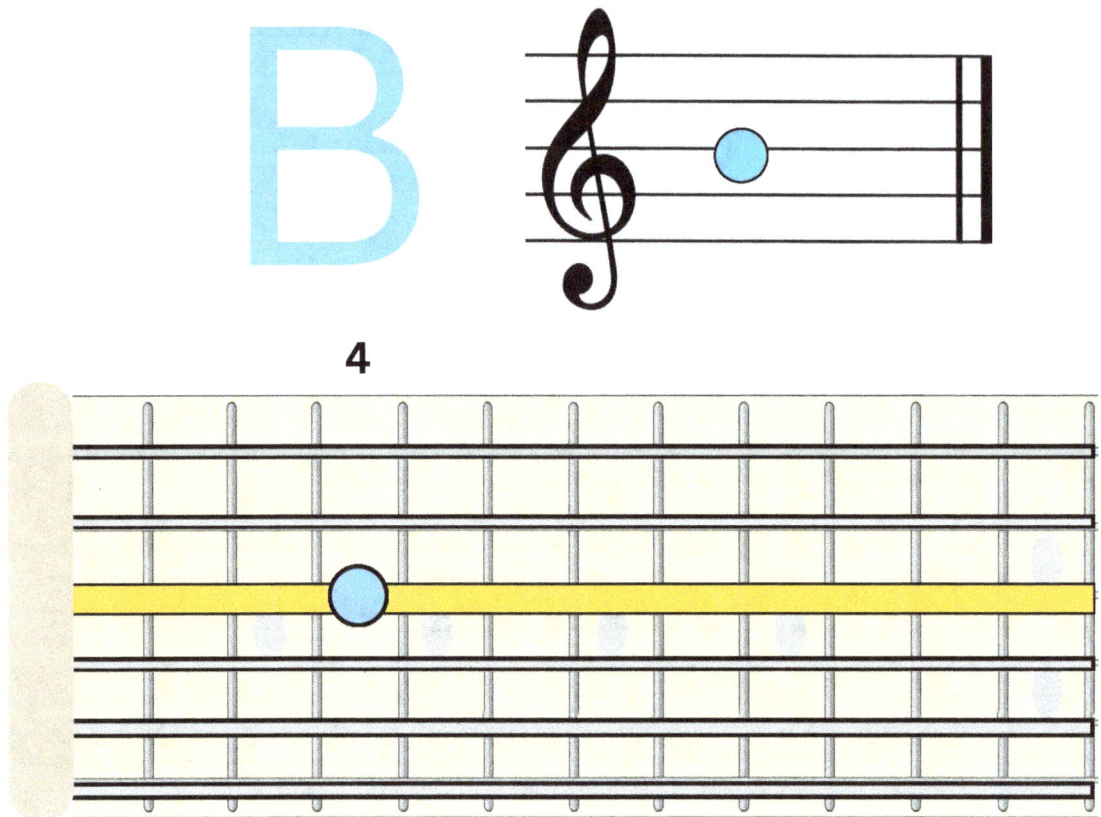

The 4th fret on the 3rd string

Go to Fret 5 for B# and Fret 3 for Bb

C

5

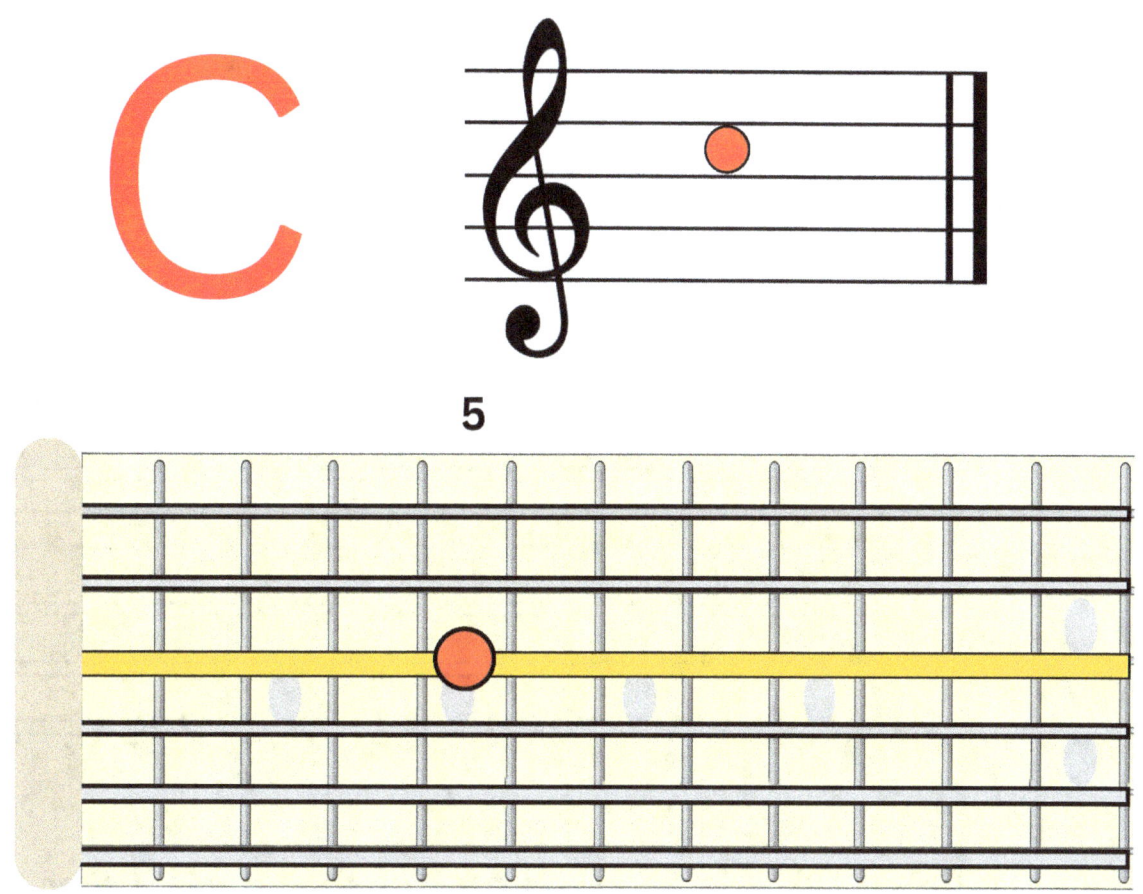

The 5th fret on the 3rd string

Go to Fret 6 for C# and Fret 4 for Cb

D

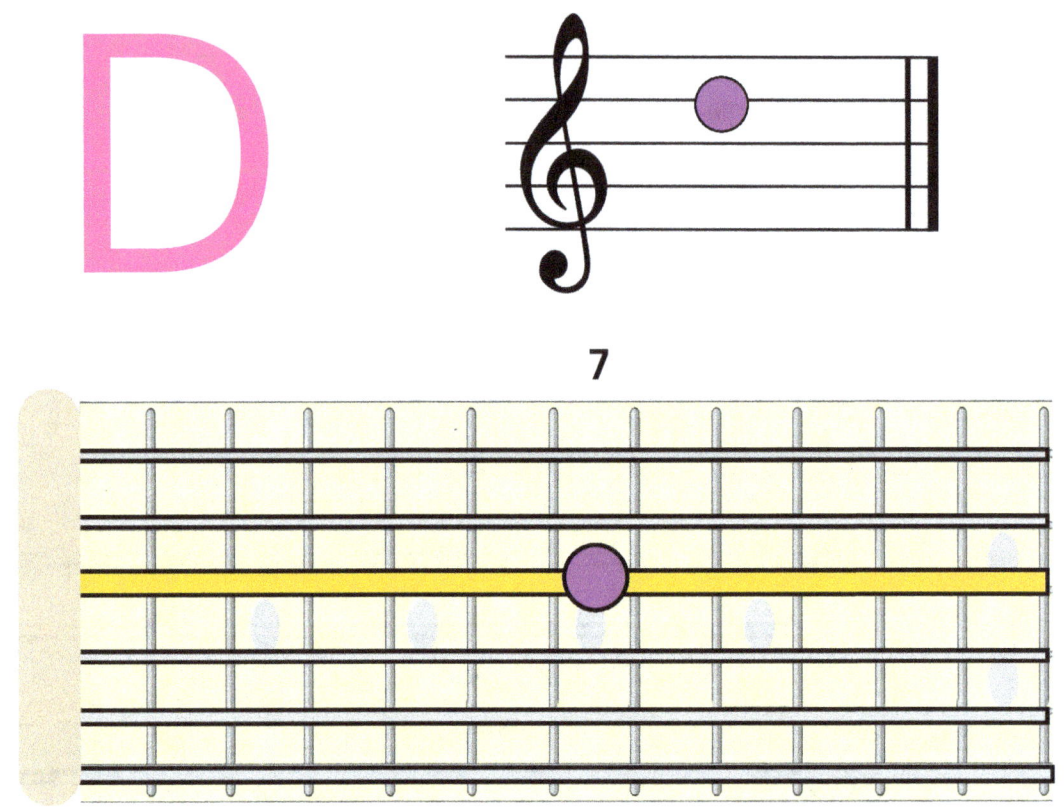

The 7th fret on the 3rd string

Go to Fret 8 for D# and Fret 6 for Db

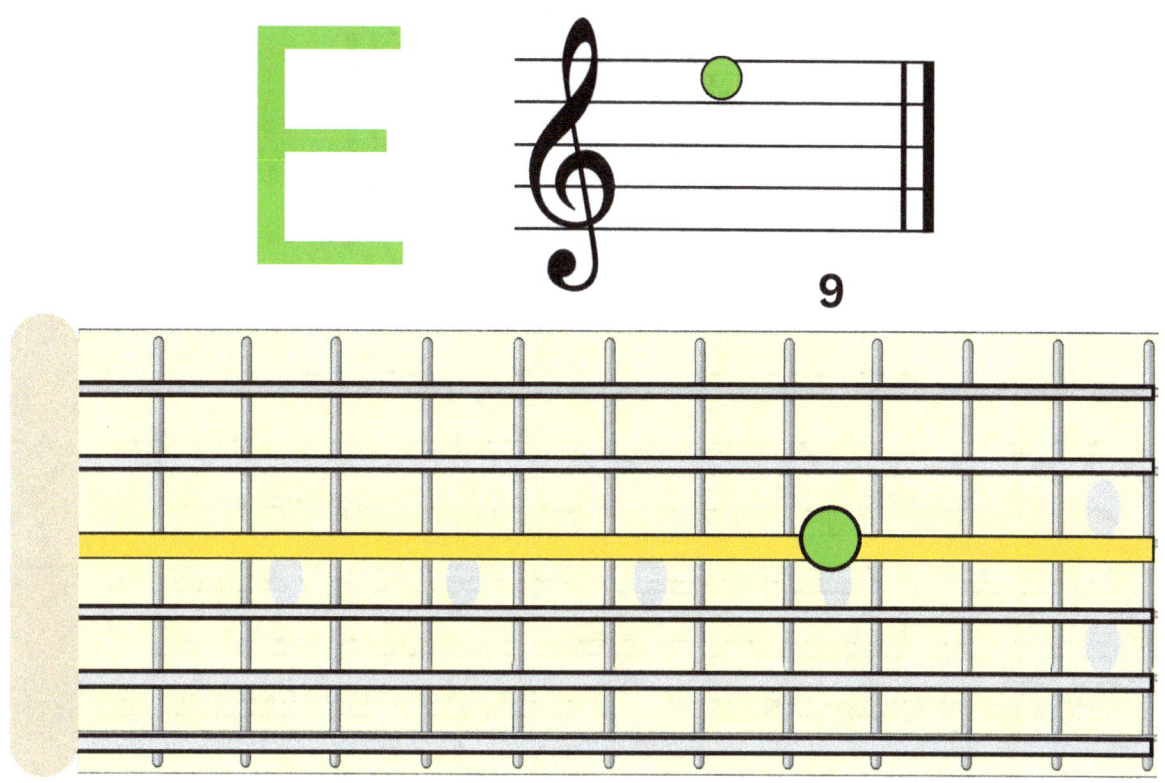

The 9th fret on the 3rd string

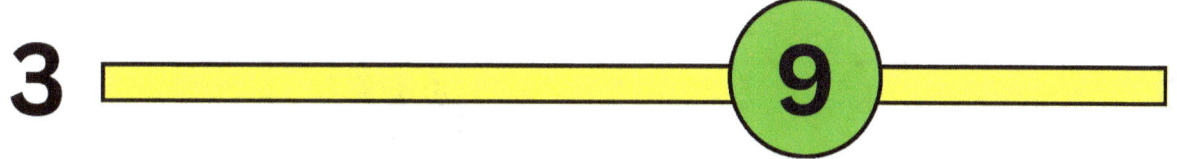

Go to Fret 10 for E# and Fret 8 for Eb

F

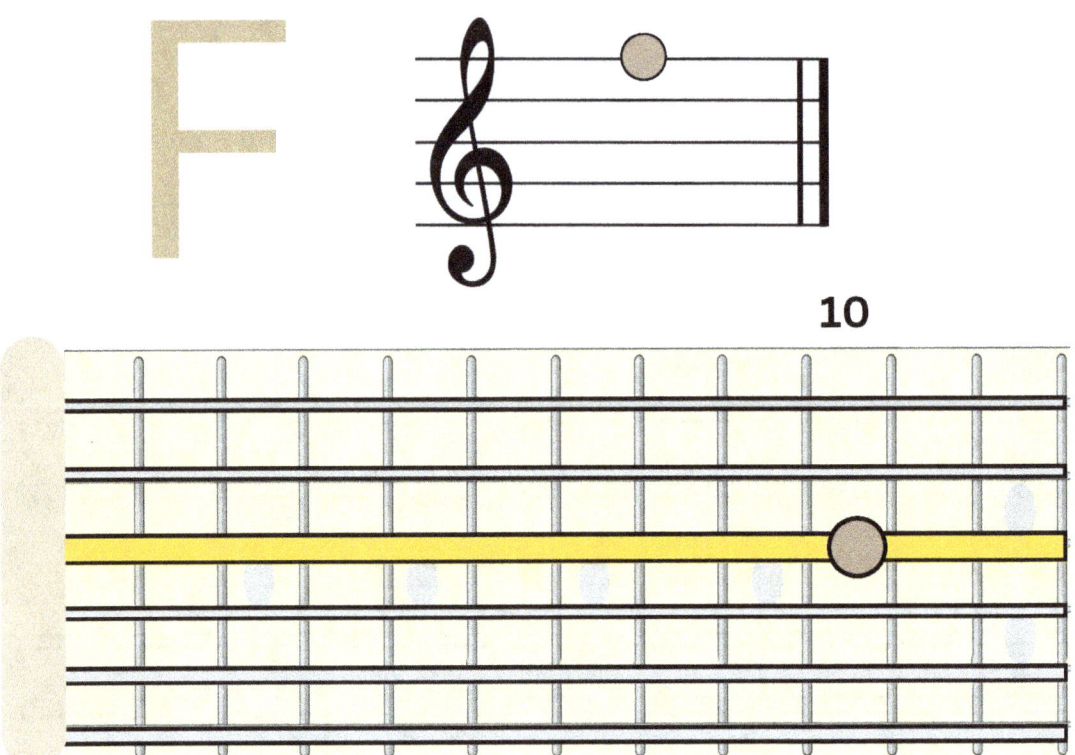

The 10th fret on the 3rd string

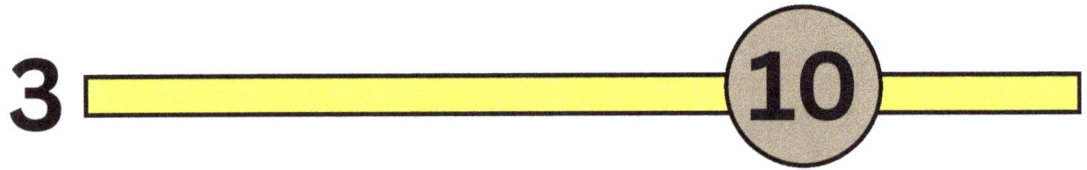

Go to Fret 11 for F# and Fret 9 for Fb

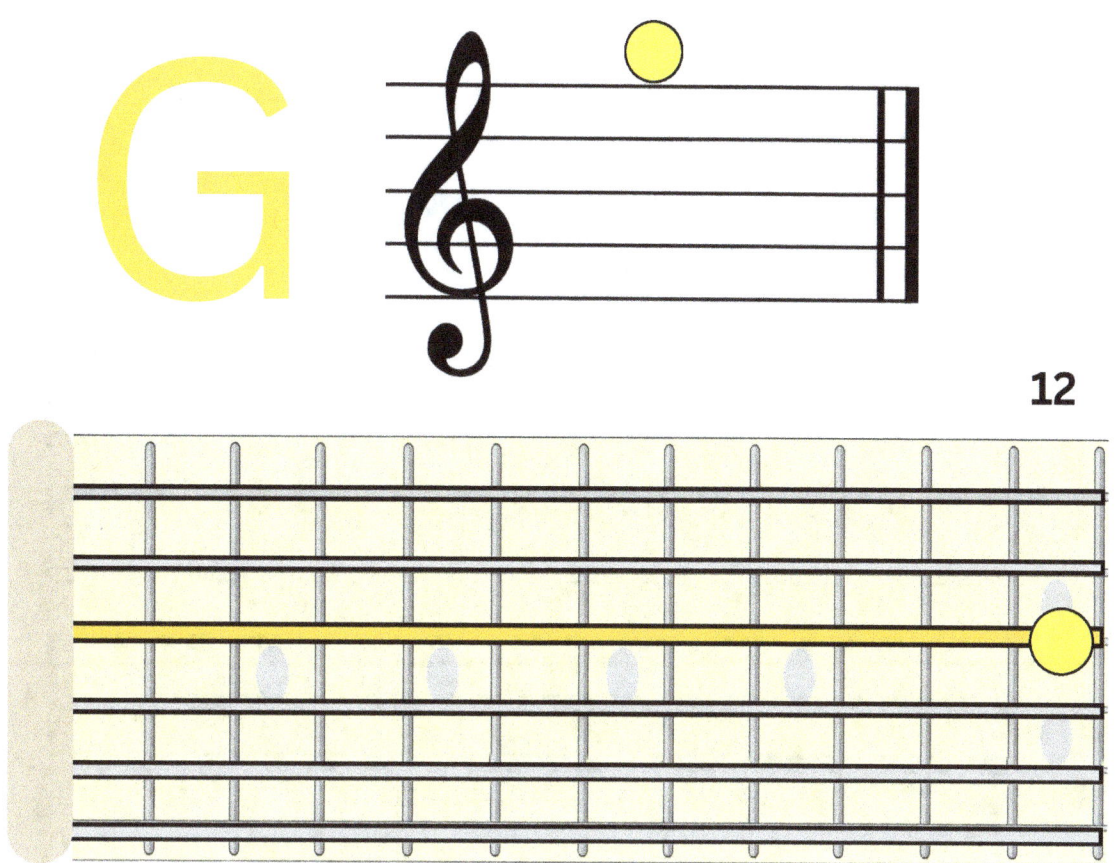

The 12th fret on the 3rd string

Go to Fret 13 for G# and Fret 11 for Gb

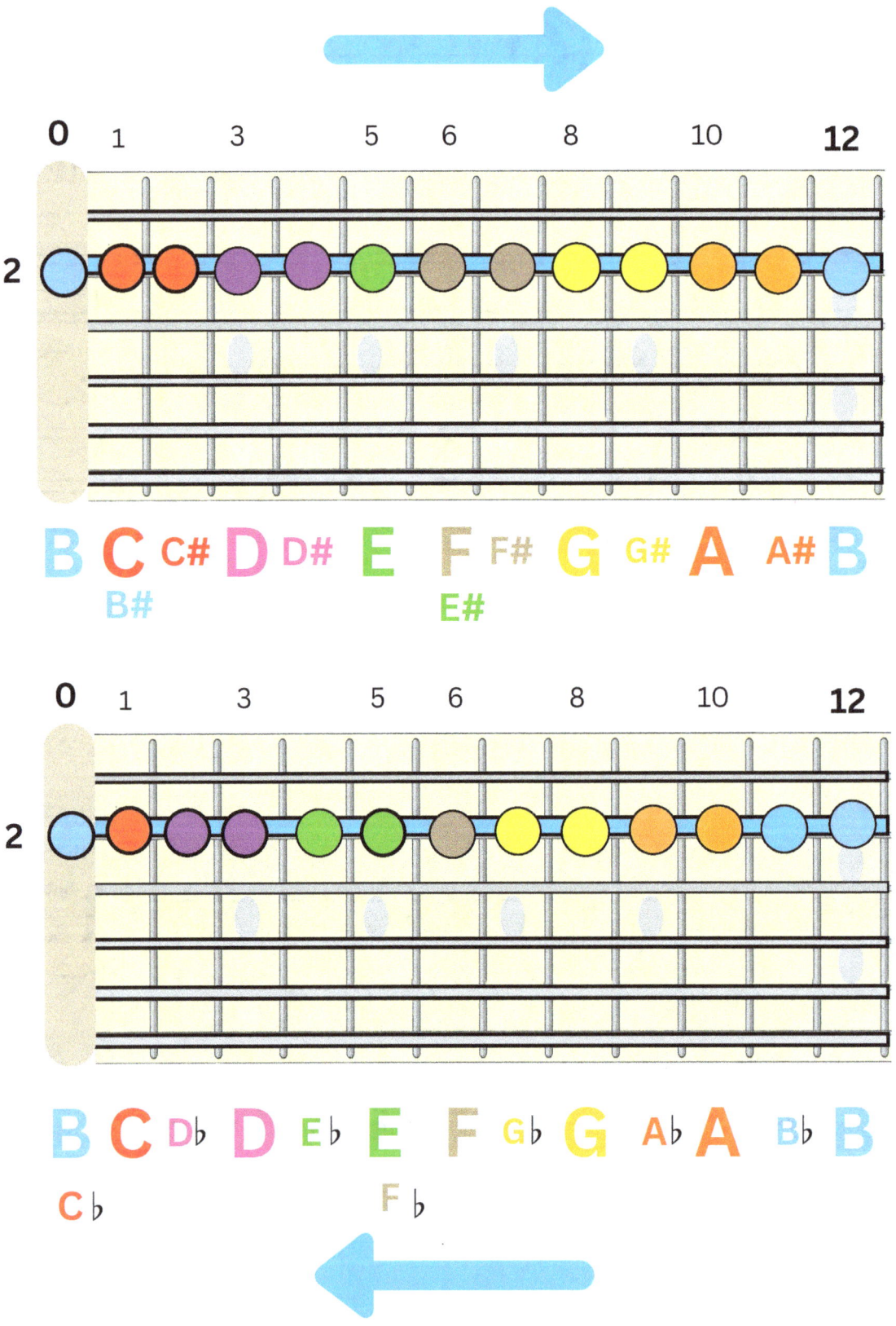

B

0

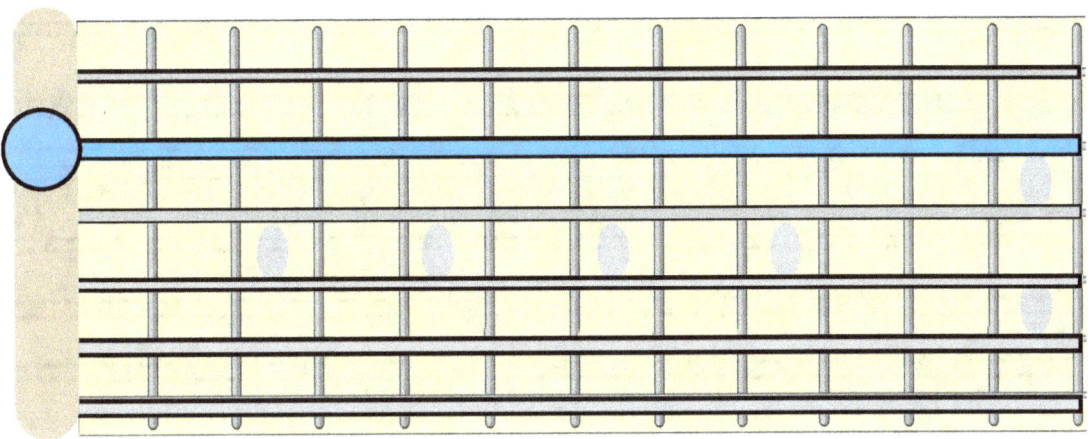

The open 2nd string

2

Go to Fret 1 for B#

C

The 1st fret on the 2nd string

Go to Fret 2 for C# and Fret 0 (open) for Cb

D

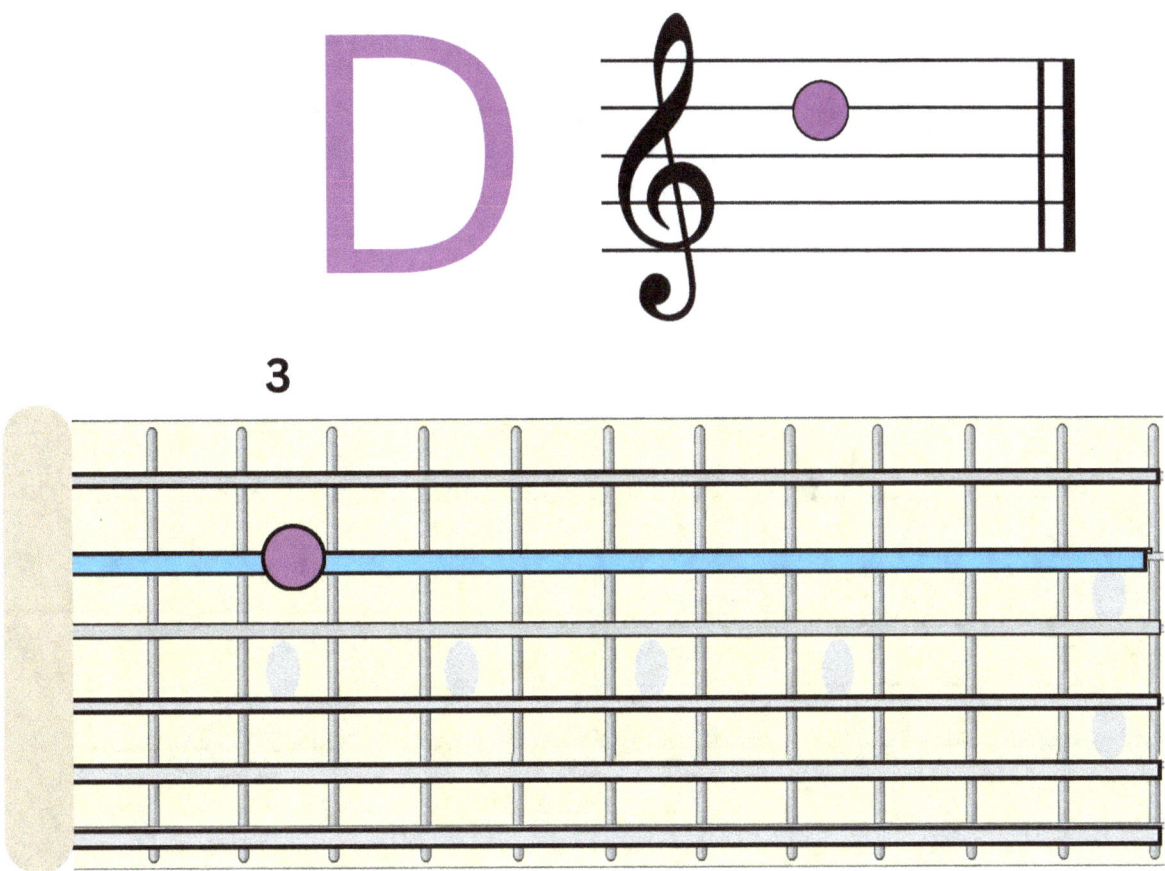

The 3rd fret on the 2nd string

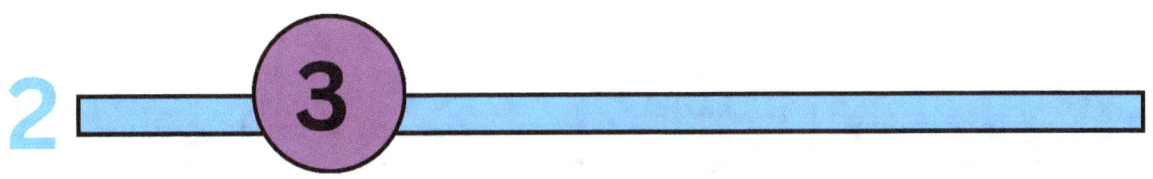

Go to Fret 4 for D# and Fret 2 for Db

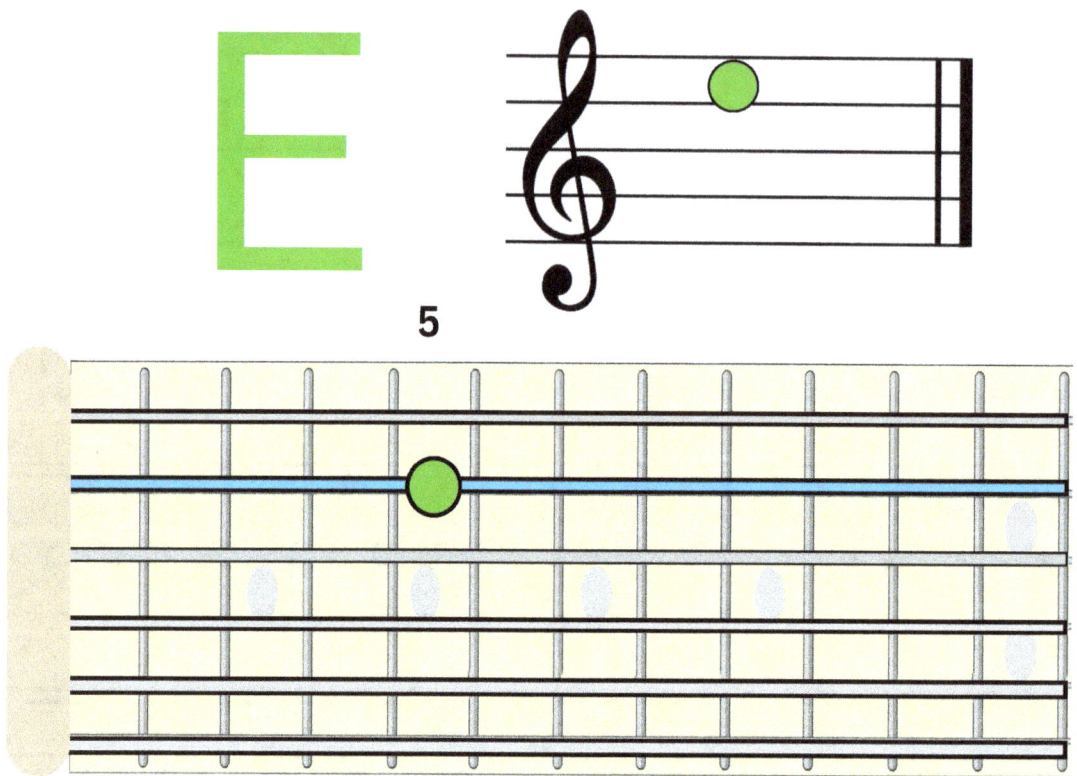

The 5th fret on the 2nd string

Go to Fret 6 for E# and Fret 4 for Eb

F

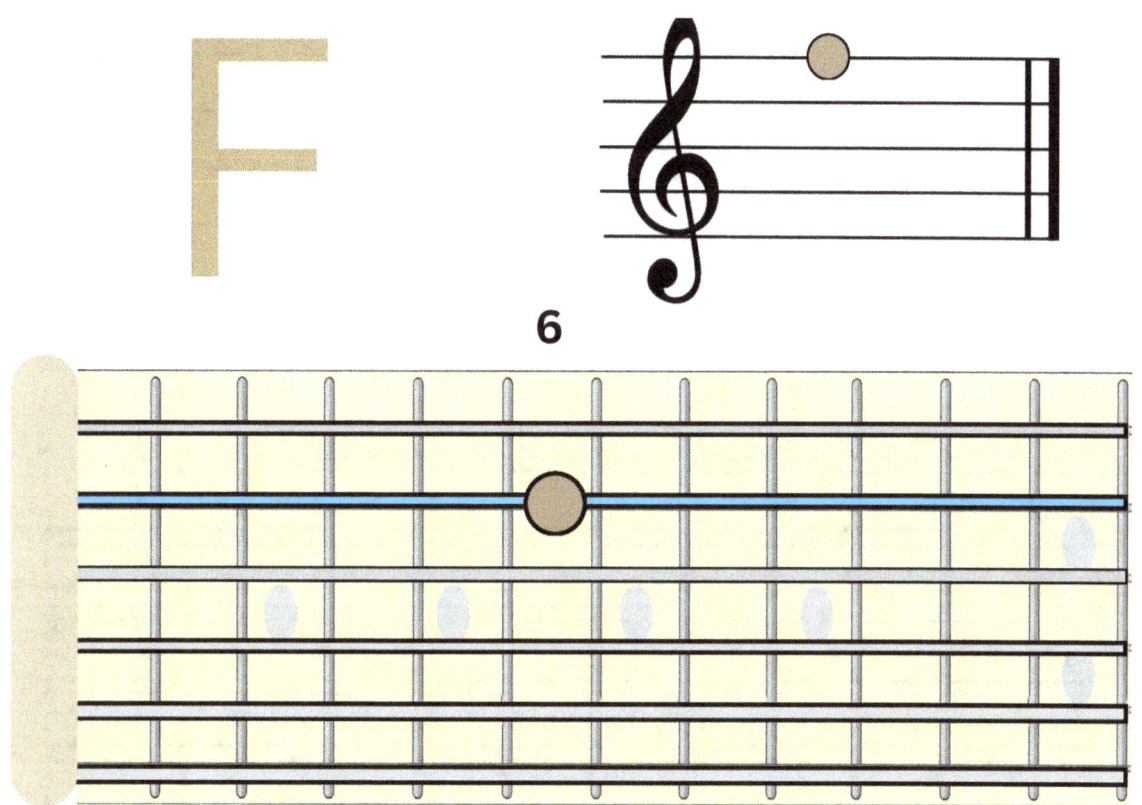

The 6th fret on the 2nd string

Go to Fret 7 for F# and Fret 5 for Fb

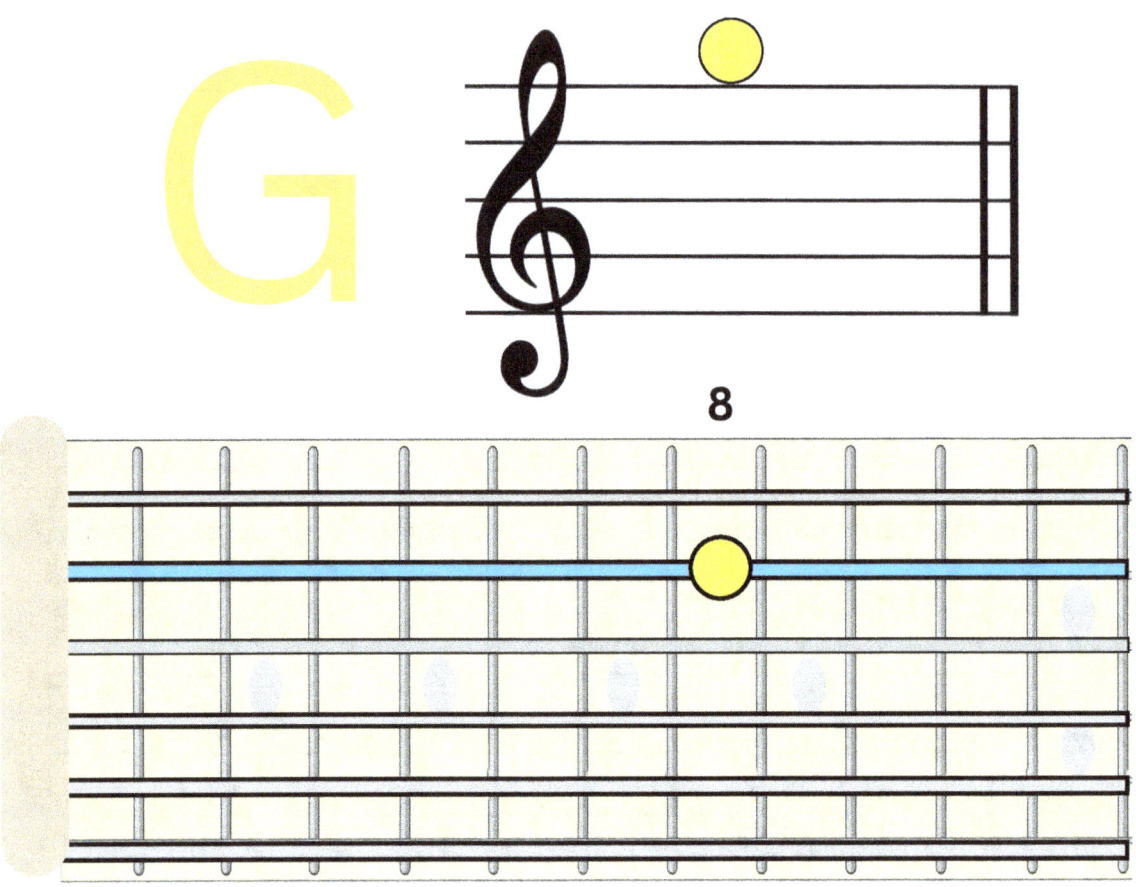

The 8th fret on the 2nd string

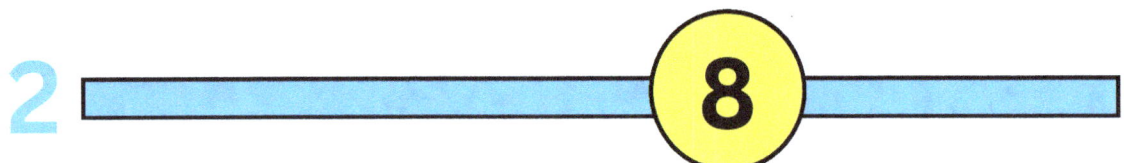

Go to Fret 9 for G# and Fret 7 for Gb

A

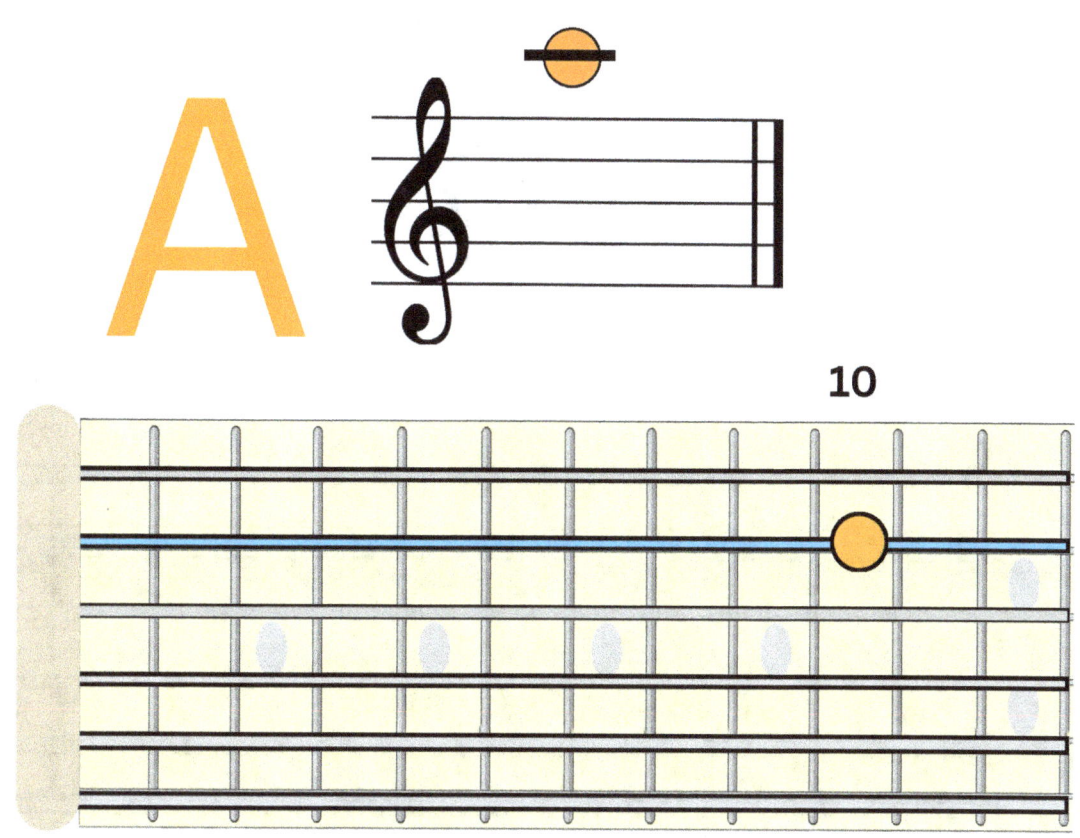

The 10th fret on the 2nd string

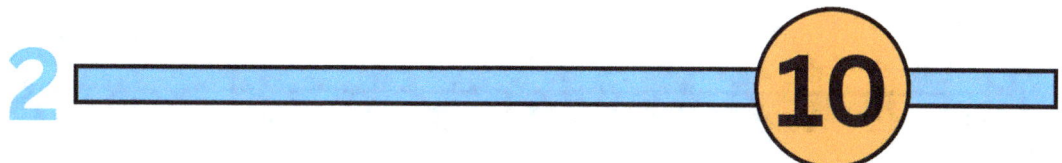

Go to Fret 11 for A# and Fret 9 for Ab

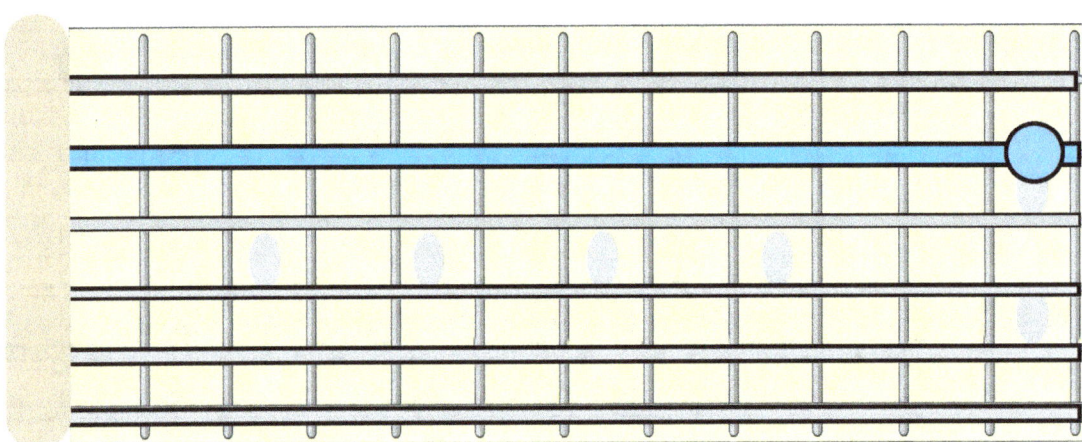

The 12th fret on the 2nd string

Go to Fret 13 for B# and Fret 11 for Bb

The 0 fret and 12th fret are Emerald as they start and end on E

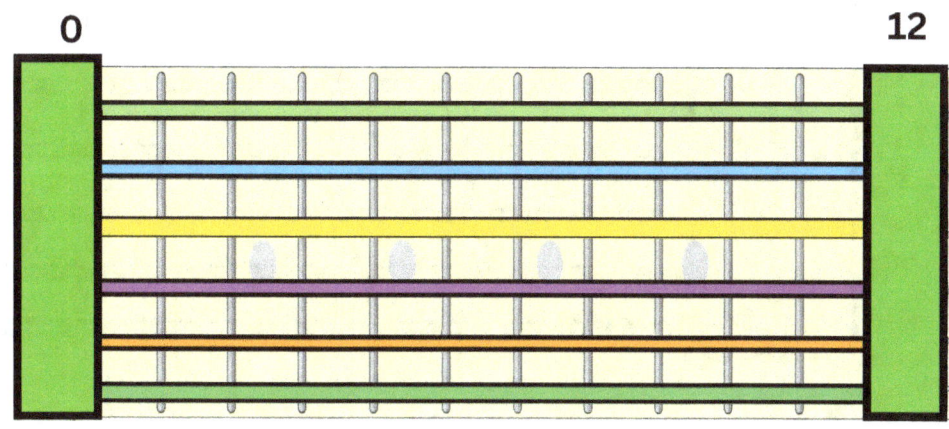

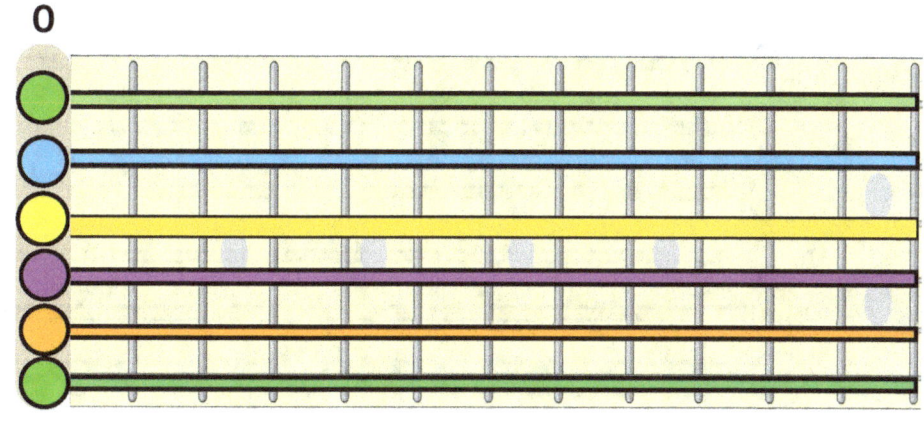

E A D G B E

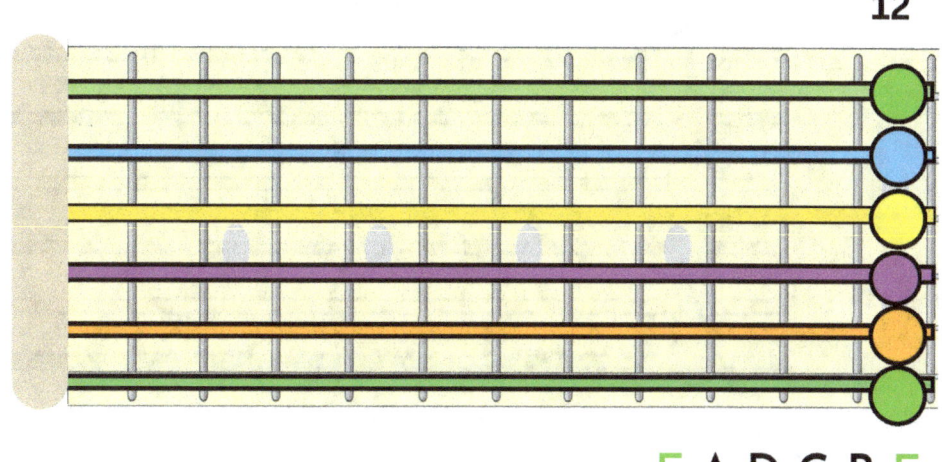

E A D G B E

The 1st and 2nd fret are Fawn

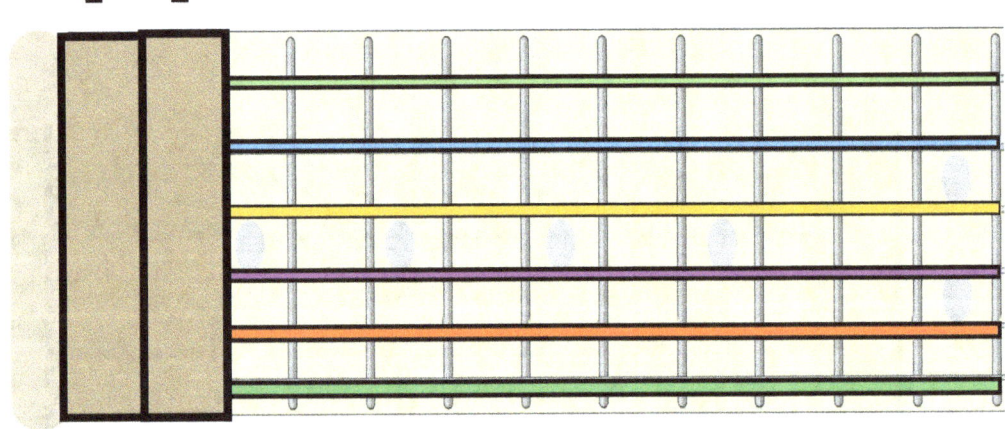

F, A#, D#, G#, C, F

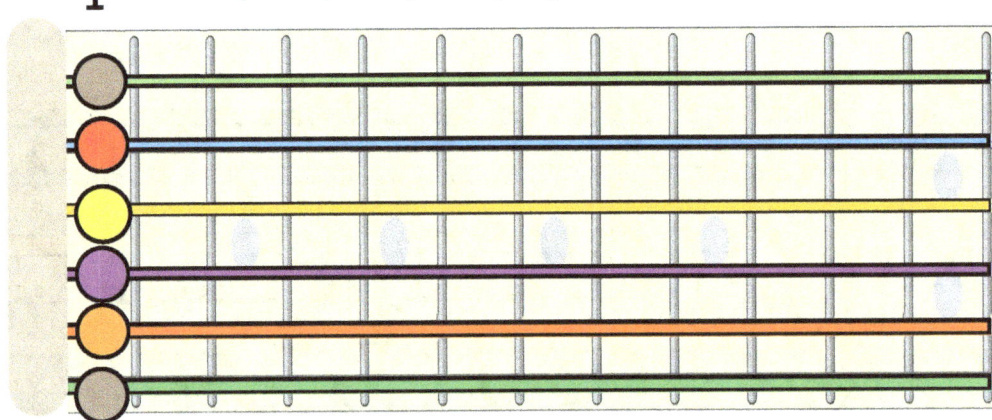

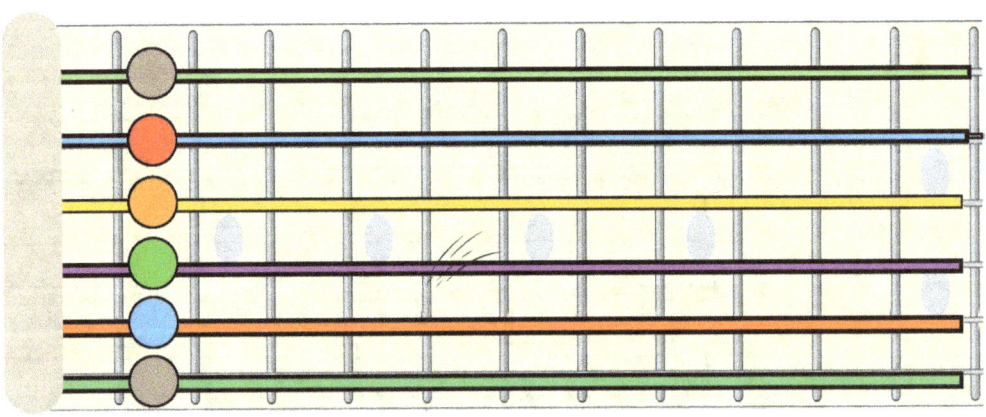

F#, B, E, A, C#, F#

The 3rd and 4th fret are Gold

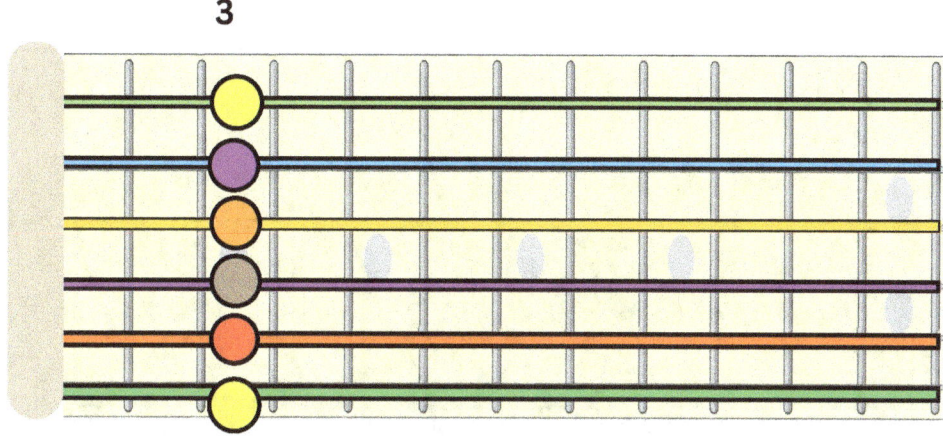

G, C, F, A#, D, G

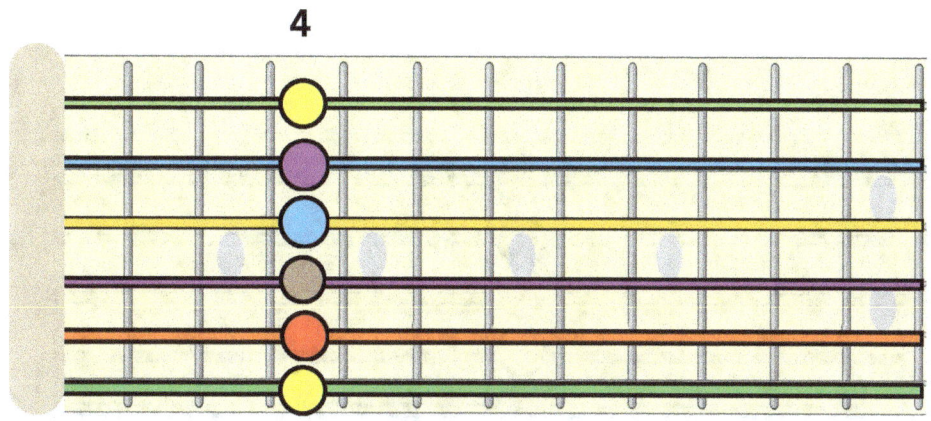

G#, C#, F#, B, D#, G#

The 5th and 6th fret are Amber

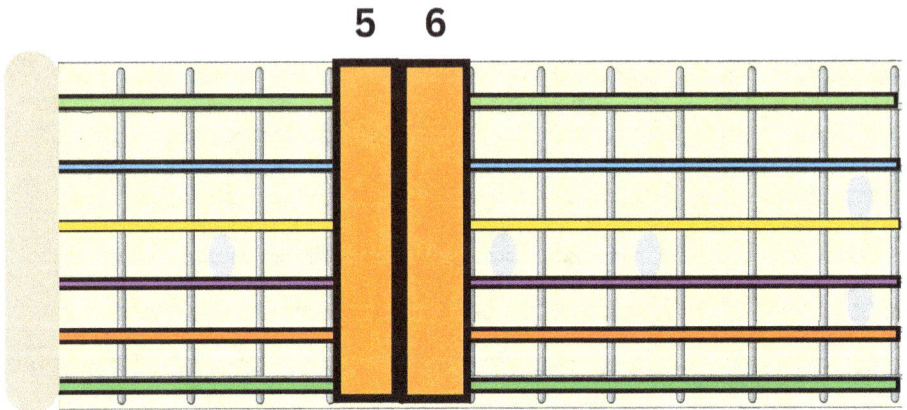

A, D, G, C, E, A

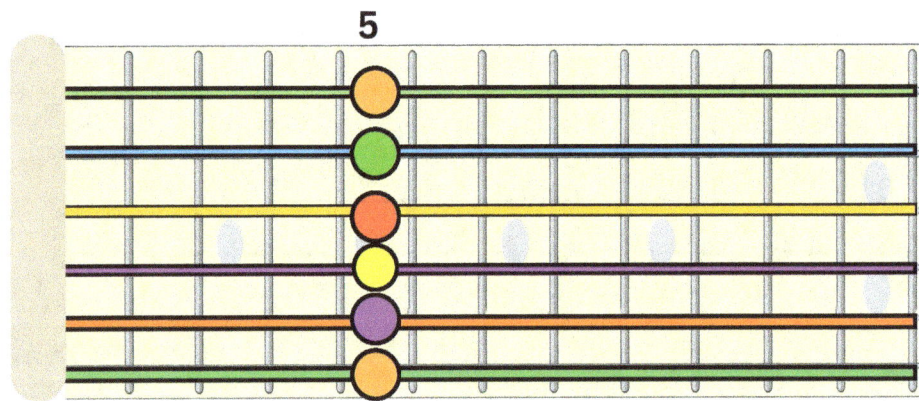

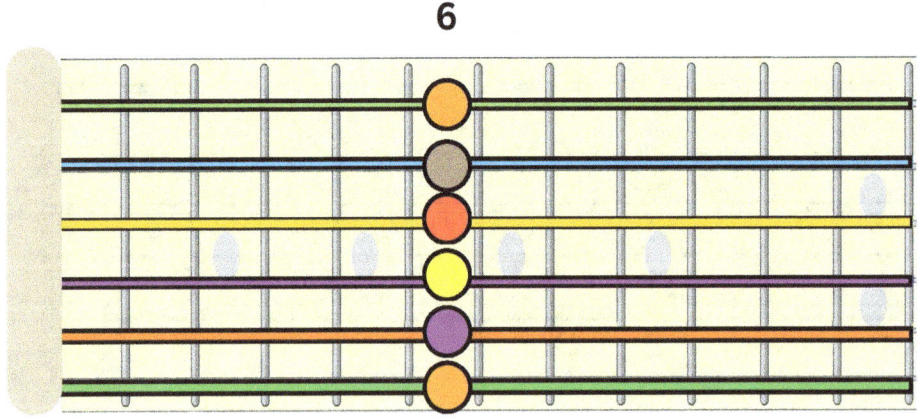

A#, D#, G#, C#, F, A#

The 7th fret is Blue

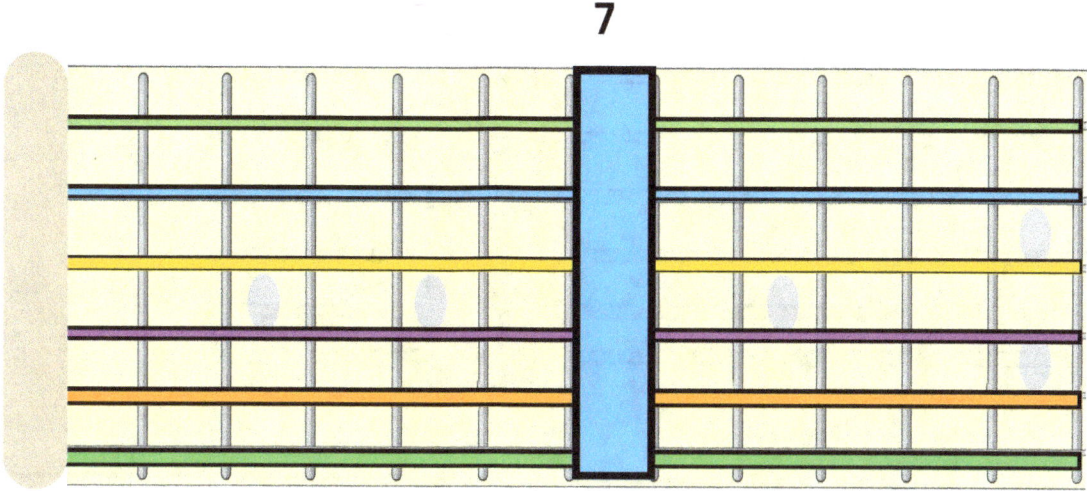

B, E, A, D, F#, B

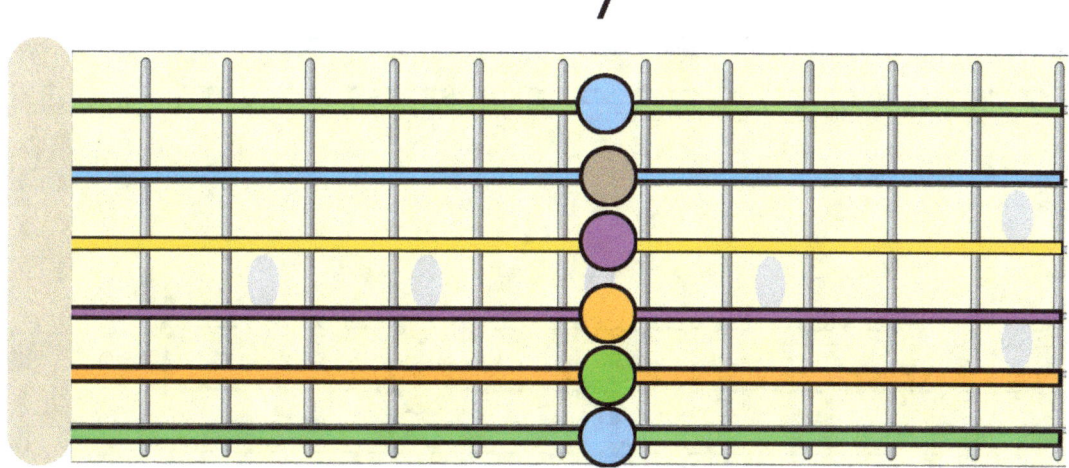

The 8th and 9th fret is Crimson

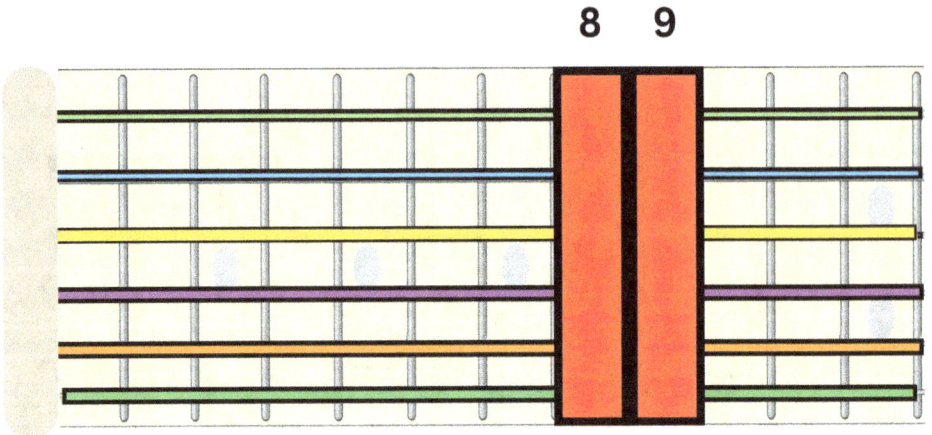

C, F, A#, D#, G, **C**

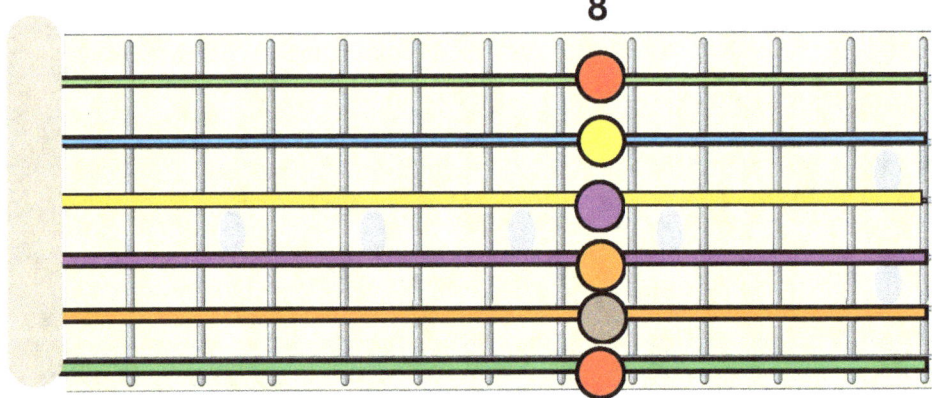

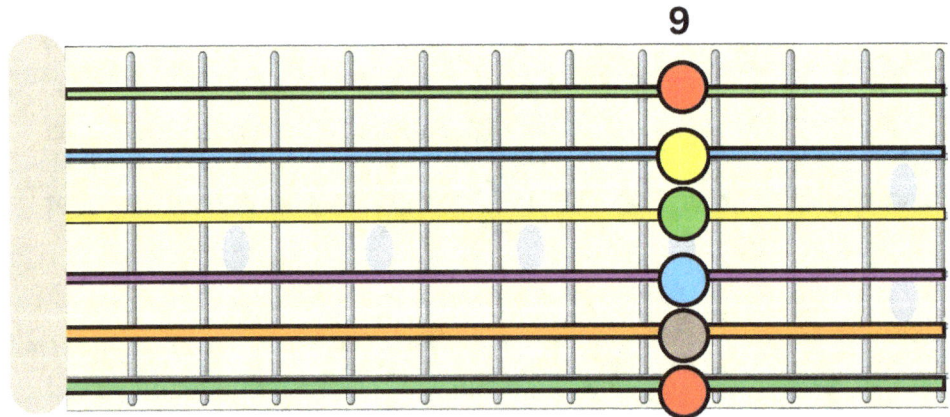

C#, F#, B, E, G#, **C#**

The 10th and 11th fret is Damson

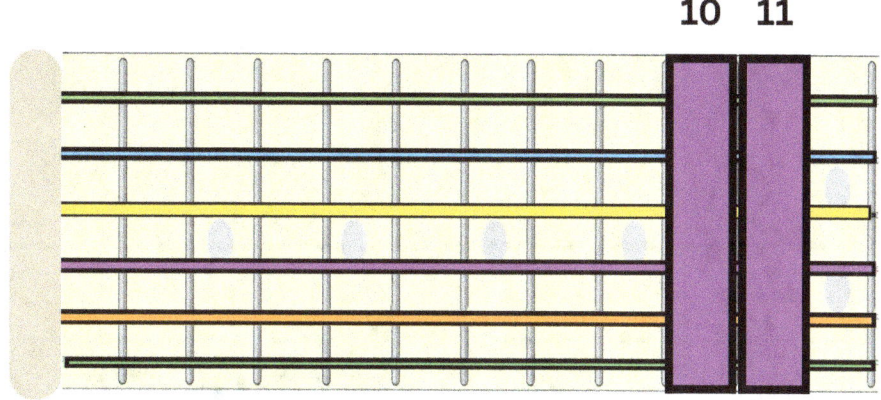

D, G, C, F, A, D

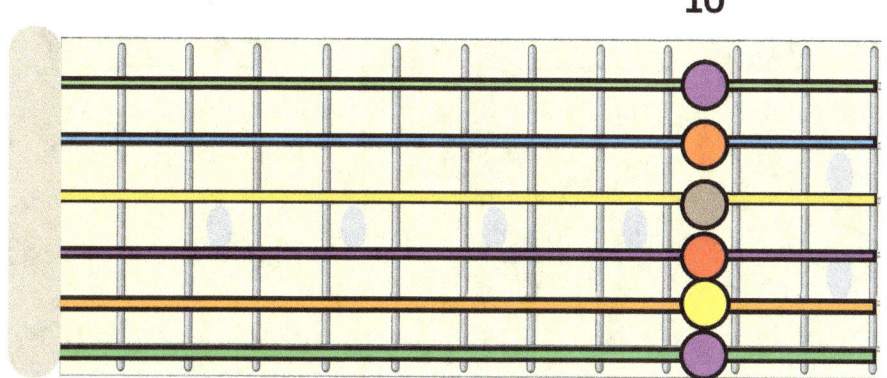

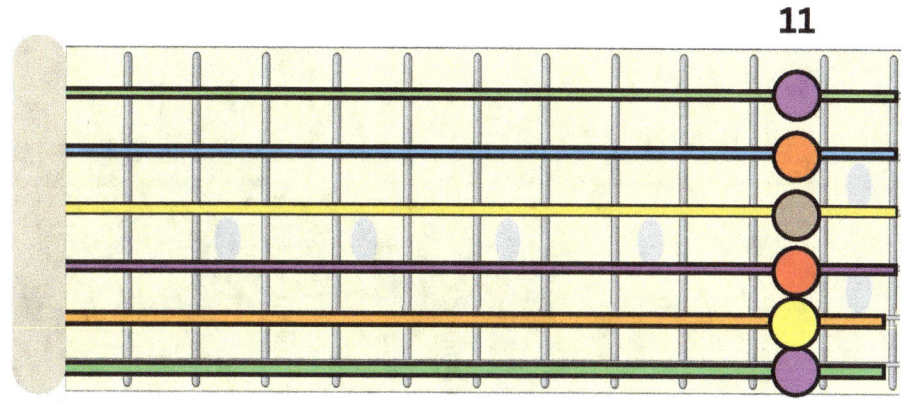

D#, G#, C#, F#, A#, D#

E - the Equestrian note

the Equestrian rides next door for Fish

WANT EXTRA MNEMONICS?
Every Good Boy Deserves Fretboard Mastery
helps with fast note mapping

E - the Equestrian note

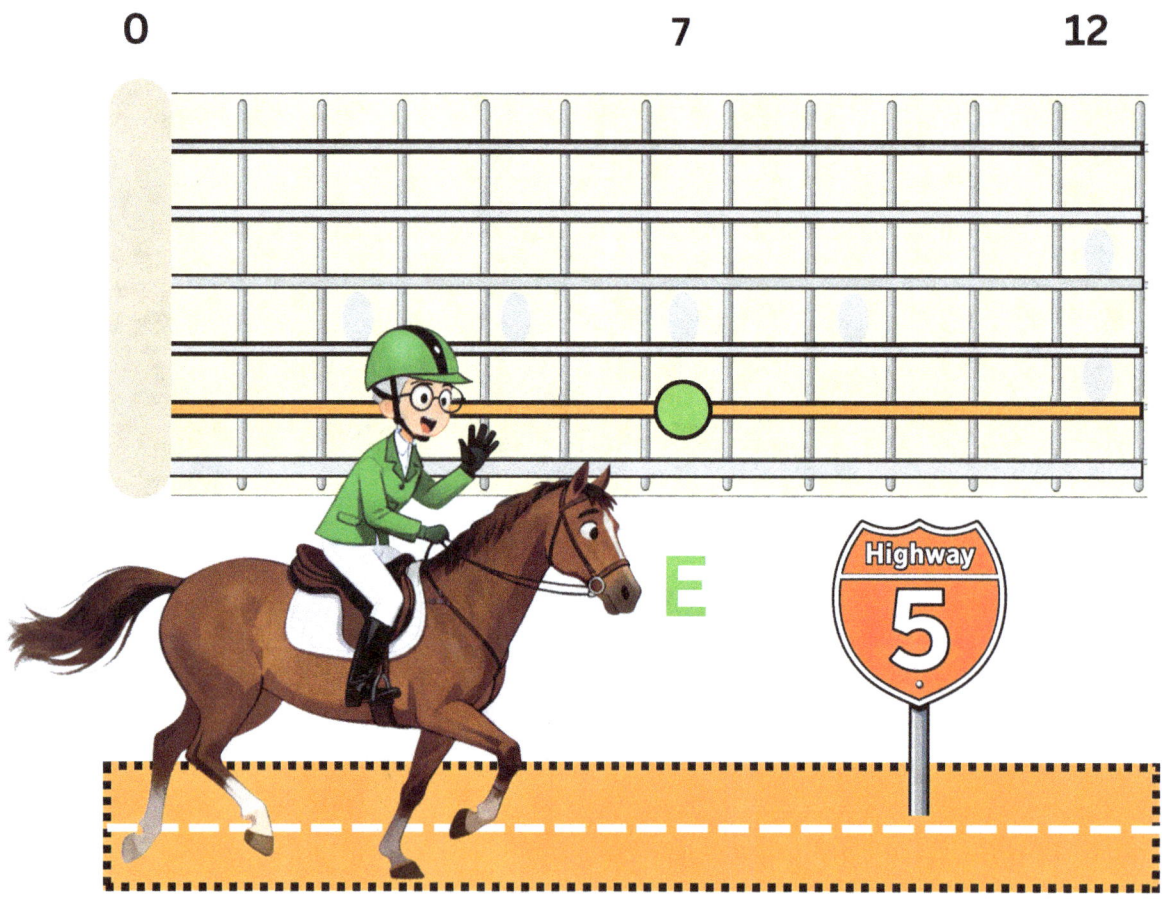

Equestrians In Devon count to 7 on the Amber Highway

Every Good Boy Deserves Fretboard Mastery
for fast fretboard mapping

B - the Bones note

Bones Jr declines to recline at 9 on the Damson Highway

Every Good Boy Deserves Fretboard Mastery
for mnemonics up and down each string

Bony **C**ats **D**ance **E**legantly, **F**lipping **G**racefully **A**round **B**oxers

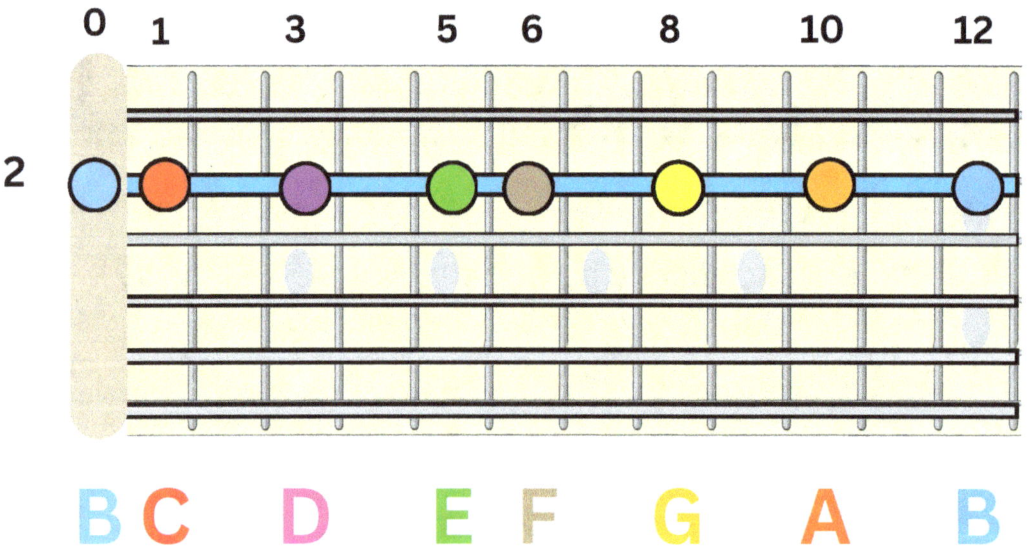

0 1 3 5 6 8 10 12

2

B C D E F G A B

Every Good Boy Deserves Fretboard Mastery for mnemonics up and down each fret

↑ **5** **A, D, G, C, E, A**

Armadillo's **D**ata **G**ot **C**lever **E**xposing **A**pricot

Armadillo works in a dive til **5**

The 5th fret is almost always marked on guitars and Armadillo's a marked man now!

www.ingramcontent.com/pod-product-compliance
Lightning Source LLC
Chambersburg PA
CBHW051421070526
44584CB00023B/3531